PAPER

MAKING

DECORATING

DESIGNING

PAPER

MAKING
DECORATING
DESIGNING

BEATA THACKERAY

SPECIAL PHOTOGRAPHY BY
JACQUI HURST

conran
OCTOPUS

To my husband Paul
and my daughter Pippa

First published in 1997 by
Conran Octopus Limited
37 Shelton Street
London WC2H 9HN

ISBN 1 85029 893 9

Commissioning Editor: Denny Hemming
Project Editor: Gillian Haslam
Art Editor: Alison Fenton
Picture Research: Jessica Walton and Jo Alexander
Production: Jill Beed and Mano Mylvaganam

British Library Cataloguing-in-Publication Data
A catalogue record for this book is available from the
British Library.

Printed and bound in China

CONTENTS

'Would that we knew how to use things such as paper as the Japanese do "with gratitude".'

SUKEY HUGHES - *WASHI*

In a world where the idea that increased mechanisation should add to the quality of our lives by extending leisure time, manual skills passed from father to son, craftsman to apprentice are disappearing fast. In our increasingly machine- and computer-reliant society, we sometimes yearn for the hand-crafted approach and hanker after the past. It is an irony that now, more than ever, we value skills that are no longer commonplace. This perhaps would explain the recent revival of many hand crafts, among them, papermaking. A huge variety of papers is made by machine, fulfilling every function imaginable, so why do we bother with a hand process which is both messy and labour-intensive? The reason is that we are fascinated with its magic and, despite all the technological advances, the hand-made product with all its character and individuality can not be replicated by purely mechanical means. Owning an object made by hand brings us more closely in contact with its maker.

The aim of this book is to demonstrate the beauty and value of this versatile material. The creative potential of a variety of hand-made papers, plus a large selection of manufactured papers, is exploited. The seemingly mundane is transformed into the visually stimulating, the scope of paper is widened and its creative potential explored, extending to all areas of design and craft to reflect the highest level of innovation and excellence.

The function of the book is not to present a list of projects to be slavishly copied. The demonstrations are about treatments rather than finished items. The hope is that you will be inspired by the many skills and processes featured and use the details given as reference points to begin your own journeys of exploration. The varied techniques shown in the book have an infinite amount of applications, allowing to you to exercise your imagination and creative flair.

In the first chapter, the world of papermaking, its history and traditions around the world are examined in brief. The emotive subject of recycling is presented with a balanced overview. The modern paper industry is considered along with a selection of the broad range of machine-made papers designed and manufactured to meet specific needs. In the second chapter, the various methods of making paper by hand are explained as the wonder of this magical process is revealed.

The third chapter demonstrates a wide range of more than twenty different techniques using paper firstly as a raw material, then as a surface for applying decoration, and finally its transformation into three-dimensional forms. Throughout this chapter, gallery pages display inspiring examples of work from artists and designers from a wide spectrum of disciplines.

I hope you will enjoy the craft of papermaking and the techniques demonstrated as much as I did when helping to compile and present them.

Right: Hand-made papermaking in the Magdi district of western Nepal. Here the centuries old tradition of pouring pulp onto a mould floated in a stream or pool is still practised to make exquisite papers of a unique texture. The wet fibres collected on the moulds are left to dry in the open air.

A SENSE OF TRADITION

'If man may now be considered as having reached a high state of civilisation his gradual development is more directly due to the inventions of paper and printing than to all other factors.'

DARD HUNTER - *Papermaking: The History and Technique of an Ancient Craft*

Paper is often valued not in its purest form but by its end use. Money, for instance, in note form, is in essence printed paper. Here we bring to light the true worth of paper, exploring traditional hand-made methods and some of the unique ingredients used. We look at the paper industry, consider the role of recycling, and examine the array of machine-made papers.

FROM RAGS TO RICHES

Despite bringing about a complete revolution in communication, little has been documented about the history of paper. Although many details remain a mystery, here are some of the key highlights, from its invention to its spread across the globe.

Before the invention of paper, many ancient civilisations were already utilising a rich variety of materials on which to transcribe their thoughts. Stone and metal were engraved, clay stamped and the bark of trees stripped and treated. The Chinese chose silk, a more flexible surface to paint on, while parchment, invented in Asia Minor in 1500 BC, was used in Europe until the sixteenth century.

Papyrus, the closest material to paper and the word from which it derives its name, is not paper by definition. First used in Ancient Egypt in around 2000 BC, the process involved laminating strips of reed, in the same way as plywood is made today.

EASTERN BEGINNINGS

The journey begins in China in AD 105, where the earliest records of paper exist. The name most commonly associated with its invention is Ts'ai Lun, the chief eunuch of the Emperor Ho-Ti. It is thought that by drawing on the existing practice of felting, experiments were conducted with offcuts of the silk used as a painting surface. This led to the use of various other plant fibres such as mulberry bark, also linked with silk manufacture.

Papermaking was brought from China to Japan via Korea in 610 by Buddhist monks. The first paper production was set up by the Emperor, and papers made from mulberry were ordered by the Imperial court. In the legendary papermaking region of Echizen, a Shinto shrine was built to honour the apparition of a deity who, according to legend, revealed the ancient craft to local people.

As the Arabian armies returned from wars in Uzbekistan in central Asia in 750, they discovered

Previous page: Lokta paper being sorted at the General Paper Industry's mill outside Kathmandu, Nepal.

Right: This photograph, taken circa 1905 at the British Paper Company's Frogmore Mill in Hemel Hempstead, shows the Fourdrinier papermaking machine. This machine, still in operation today, is a direct development of the first Fourdrinier machine installed at Frogmore Mill in 1803.

that some of their captives knew the secret of making paper with plant fibres. The use of flax fibre and linen rags was introduced to Arabia and the first paper mill established in Bagdad by Caliph Harun-al-Rashid in 794.

WESTERN TRADITIONS

Wherever they conquered new lands, the Arabic Moslems built paper mills, first in Cairo, Egypt, in 900, then in Morocco and Sicily in 1100, before reaching Spain in 1144 .

The linen method of papermaking was brought to Central and Northern Europe by the veterans of the Crusades. Over a thousand years after its invention in the Orient, the craft finally became established in Europe as the first paper mills began to appear in 1260 in Fabriano, Italy; in 1348 in France; in 1390 in Nuremburg, Germany; in 1491 in Krakow, Poland; 1495 in Hertford, England and by 1576 in Moscow. By the seventeenth century papermaking had become established in Scandinavia. The first American paper mill appeared in 1690 in Germantown, Pennsylvania.

During the eighteenth century, as printing methods were developed and demand for paper grew, the rags traditionally used for the production of paper were in short supply. As prices increased, hence the phrase 'from rags to riches', the mills began to experiment with cheaper alternatives.

In 1719 the French naturalist and physicist René Antoine Ferchault de Réaumur discovered the secret held by the Canadian wasp. Investigating how the wasp built its nest, he noticed that it chewed wood slivers and, with its saliva, sized the substance and spread it on its nest, creating a paper-like covering.

In 1801 Matthias Koops set up the first commercial mill in the West, producing paper without rags, deriving his fibres from wood, bark and other plant sources. In America, straw was used as the first alternative fibre source to rags and commercial manufacture was set up by mill owner G. Shyrock. Strawpaper and board led to a revolution in the packaging of commerical goods with strawboard used to make the first paper boxes.

Nevertheless, wood was to become the industry's primary source for the production of pulp. In 1867, at exhibitions in Paris and London, Friederich Keller and Heinrich Voelter displayed a new machine for grinding wood into pulp. The thin, cheap paper made from this pulp revolutionised the spread of information as it was used for newspapers and, for this reason, was known as newsprint. At this time, experiments were being conducted in America and Sweden to perfect a process by which wood could be broken down by boiling. By the 1890s the chemical sulphite method began to be employed by mills in Europe and America.

EARLY MECHANISATION

In 1680 a Dutch invention revolutionised pulp production by drastically cutting the time it took to reduce rags to fibres. The Hollander Beater, comprising a large wooden tub with a revolving roller fitted with cutting blades, ground the rags against a stone plate. Although rags are no longer the main ingredient in papermaking, this form of beater is still used across the globe to this day.

The first papermaking machine was invented by Nicolas-Louis Robert in 1799 at Essones in France. In England the Fourdrinier brothers funded the development of a more sophisticated model, based on Robert's plans. The first commercial Fourdrinier machine was installed at Frogmore Mill, Hertforshire, by 1803. It was now possible to make paper of unrestricted length, the width being determined only by the size of the machine. This milestone achievement was to transform the manufacture of paper throughout the West. The fact that paper could now be made on a roll greatly influenced the development of modern printing methods with the introduction of rotary presses.

Above: The Canadian wasp can be regarded as the first real papermaker as for eons it has chewed on slivers of wood and lined its nest with a pulp-like matter.

Right: 'Shibori' or oil-treated papers with the appearance of leather were used for over-shoes and tobacco pouches. Made of a number of laminated sheets soaked in oil, these papers were pressed onto wooden blocks to achieve a distinct surface texture and then printed using stencils.

Right: This is 'gikakushi', or imitation leather paper, from the Edo period when Buddhist belief discouraged the killing of animals. Dampened kozo paper was pressed into blocks of carved cherry wood and then treated with oil or lacquer. It was used for boxes, book covers and furniture panels, while in Europe it was used as wallpaper.

Right: Made from coloured kozo and mitsumata (two of the main pulp ingredients in Japanese papermaking), this paper was used for 'fusuma' or sliding doors. Known as 'taiheishi' or pacific paper, it is thought that the deep furrows in the surface were created during the formation of the sheet when the mould was shaken vigorously.

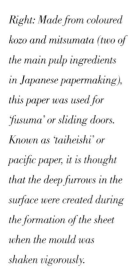

THE PARKES' COLLECTION

Arguably the world's most precious collection of historical papers, The Parkes' Collection is stored at the Victoria & Albert Museum and The Royal Botanical Gardens at Kew in London. It dates back to the nineteenth century and is named after Sir Harry Smith Parkes, the British Consul in Japan from 1865 to 1883. Sir Harry researched the papermaking regions of Japan and compiled a comprehensive collection of over 2,500 papers and articles from 21 prefectures. This work is of particular value as it dates from the most prestigious period of Japanese papermaking when the Imperial Court nurtured the development of the craft, and was responsible for defining its principles.

The collection, together with its documentation, was transported to England in 1871 where it lay undisturbed and forgotten until 1978. Until then, the only evidence of this collection existed in the form of a photocopy of the documentation, held in Japan where it was thought that the highly prized papers and articles had been lost. Thanks to the interest of Hans and Tanya Schmoller, its existence was highlighted and the articles reappraised. This discovery made headline news in Japan. The collection was loaned to Japan in 1994 for an exhibition, attracting around 30,000 visitors. Detailed research is currently under way to examine their method of manufacture as well as structure.

Right: 'Kanoko' or crepe paper and 'shiborizome' tie-dyed papers were used as hair decorations by women of the poorer classes who could not afford the silk versions. The creping was achieved by pressing damp paper between carved planks. The fine tie-dye was created with bamboo splints pressed into the paper at regular points, the paper tied off and the splints removed before dyeing. These examples are rare as this type of adornment was often discarded after use.

TRADITIONS AROUND THE WORLD

Below: At the Udyog Paper Project in Bangladesh the Oriental method of papermaking is practised, whereby paper is formed on a flexible bamboo screen. Once the sheet is couched, the screen is peeled away, leaving behind the layer of fibres ready for pressing.

There are two distinct methods for hand papermaking geographically divided between the East and West, with only slight regional variations.

WESTERN PAPERMAKING

The Western method uses a mesh-covered mould and a deckle (see page 36) which are held together and dipped into a vat containing a mixture of water and pulp. As they are lifted, the fibres disperse evenly over the mesh and are couched onto a board.

Interleaved with felt, the sheets create a pile known as a 'post'. This is placed in a screw press and the water is squeezed out several times. The sheets are then peeled away and hung to dry individually. In hand-made paper mills the process is carried out by the 'vatman' and the 'coucher', working together as a synchronised team. The sheets are then laid on beds or hung to dry in special drying lofts before being pressed flat.

ORIENTAL PAPERMAKING

The Japanese papermaking method differs in many ways. Longer fibres are used, most commonly derived from plants such as *kozo*, *gampi* and *mitsumata* and are prepared with great care so that all impurities are meticulously removed. A substance known as *neri*, resembling glue, is added to the vat, thickening the water and slowing down the drainage. It also allows the sheets to be couched on top of one another without the need for interleaving. Surprisingly, the sheets do not bond together, even after pressing.

Rather than a mesh-covered rigid frame, this method uses a flexible bamboo screen or *su* on which the fibres are collected. The screen rests on a wooden frame or *geta* which is hinged by a system of overhead pulleys. The screen and frame are scooped in the vat and, unlike the Western method whereby the thickness of the paper is determined by the consistency of the slurry, the layers are built up as the screen is dipped several times. The Oriental method of pressing the paper takes many hours, using either weights applied on top of the post or a press operated by a lever to which pressure is gradually applied. The sheets are pasted on boards of seasoned wood and dried in the open air.

The papermakers I have worked with in Kathmandu employ the Japanese method with awe-inspiring skill. However, the traditional method in the Himalayan countries of Nepal and Bhutan resembles the one originally used by the Chinese.

Left: Papermaking using lokta fibre, derived from the indigenous tree harvested throughout the western middle hills of the Magdi district in western Nepal. This traditional paper-making process resembles the early Chinese method and is carried out by more than 300 families of the Hindu Chetri caste. The paper is sold locally and to the larger markets in Kathmandu.

A mould is lowered into a shallow pool of water onto which pulp is poured. The mould is lifted and the fibres are left on the mesh to dry.

The technique traditionally employed in India to make cotton rag paper resembles the Japanese method, using a flexible bamboo screen or *chhapri* and a wooden frame or *sacha*. The most interesting point of difference is the construction of the vat which is sunk into the floor. The papermaker or *kagzi* crouches on a platform or stands in a recess, the base of the vat forming a deep slope. Freestanding metal vats are also used, some with overhead pulleys and levers to take the weight of the frame. The paper is pasted on external walls to dry and the sheets vigorously polished using glass or conch shells to remove impurities.

Making paper by hand is a precious art still practised in many parts of the world, and each individual papermaking region has a different story to tell.

JAPAN

For centuries the Japanese have used paper for an inexhaustible list of everyday articles. They have worn it, lived in it and even killed with it.

Some kimonos were made of sheets of paper or a woven paper fabric called *shifu*. In traditional Japanese houses the window panes and internal sliding panels or *shoji* are made of paper. *Washi*, Japanese hand-made paper, has been used to kill by suffocation with a wet sheet laid over the victim's mouth. During the Second World War, a huge nationwide project was undertaken to make paper for the construction of bomb-carrying balloons.

The papermaker was traditionally regarded as a living treasure but, as with many crafts, the practice is in decline. The number of households making paper has dropped from hundreds of thousands in the mid nineteenth century (before the introduction of the Western papermaking machine) to below a thousand since the 1950s.

Right: The ancient papermaking traditionally practised in Bhutan has almost disappeared due to mass importation of cheaper papers from India. However, these less durable machine-made papers are unsuited to the needs of the monks who use paper to print religious texts, and some hand papermaking practices have been revived using Japanese techniques to enhance traditional methods. The Tshasho process shown here is used to form thick sheets on a flexible bamboo mould placed on a crude wooden framework. The paper-maker sits on a bench with a well for his feet and leans forward, dipping the mould into the vat. Sheets are couched on a post without any need for interleaving.

CHINA

In China, papermaking remains a highly revered craft with some locations kept secret. The skill commands respect as it was originally used to transcribe the sayings of ancient philosophy and religion. A paper named *Hong Xing*, meaning the best paper made in China, is used by professional calligraphers and painters in China and Japan.

INDIA

Papermaking was first introduced to Kashmir in the mid fifteenth century by the Moghuls, although there are earlier accounts of its existence in India. It was primarily the Muslims who practised the craft, travelling as far south as Maharashtra to set up manufacture. The British Government was responsible for almost wiping out the practice in 1840 when the Secretary of State for India ordered that all paper used by the Government be bought from Britain. The money lenders or *sawkar* are credited with having saved the craft, as they alone continued to use the paper for their account books.

A revival took place in the 1930s as Mahatma Ghandi encouraged traditional village crafts. Today a few papermaking centres still exist, supplying the Indian Government with hand-made paper, although some modern methods have been introduced to make it more commercially viable.

EUROPE

Over the last twenty years making paper by hand has generated increasing attention in the West. As it is now practised primarily as a craft, few commercial operations exist today. In eighteenth-century England there were as many as 115 mills making paper by hand, located mainly in the southeast. Today there are a handful of makers selling their product to specialist markets, such as conservation, book restoration and painting. The Two Rivers Paper Company in Somerset is a commercial papermaking operation run by Jim

Patterson who produces four tonnes of high quality watercolour paper each year. The famous paper factory at Wookey Hole in Somerset, now a working museum, fulfils orders from as far away as Korea.

Across central and southern Europe there are very few working mills. Among the seven mills in France, some are commercial and one is a museum, while in Italy the famous Fabriano mill still sells a hand-made range. There is a working mill and museum in Italy and also in Spain, and individual Swiss and German papermakers offer workshops.

Papers made at Ruscombe Mill and supplied by JvO Papers have a particular significance. Produced for specialist conservation, each sheet is made to emulate historic papers dating back over 200 years. The unique specimens are studied for fibre content and method of manufacture while the original dyes are computer matched. This allows rare papers to be recreated in their exact detail.

AMERICA AND CANADA

A revival in hand-made paper began in the 1960s, continuing into the 1970s. Many of the mills were set up by artists making paper for their own use and for printmakers and painters. Many small mills exist today across North America and Canada, notably the Twinrocker Mill in Indiana, set up in 1973.

Above: Paper being formed at the General Paper Industries' mill in Kathmandu, Nepal. Traditional Oriental bamboo screens are used to collect the fibres. The screen is held over the vat to allow the water to drain away as the skilled papermaker prepares to couch the newly formed sheet.

ALTERNATIVE FIBRE SOURCES

Why should we consider using alternative fibres for papermaking when wood pulp has served us so well? Bernadette Vallely, former Executive Director of The Women's Environmental Network (WEN), believes that by the year 2050, trees will no longer be the main raw material for paper.

A Gallup Poll carried out in 1990 revealed that 70 per cent of the people questioned believed that the paper industry was responsible for the destruction of the tropical rainforests. However, the industry states that tropical wood is not used for papermaking as it is fundamentally unsuitable for the manufacturing process. According to The Paper and Pulp Information Centre, only 12 per cent of the trees felled worldwide are used by the paper industry, while the main source of wood pulp comes from forest thinnings and the waste from saw mills.

The source of 94 per cent of wood used by the European paper industry is sustainably managed forests of Europe, where softwoods such as pine and spruce and a smaller amount of hardwoods such as birch and eucalyptus are grown. Although the trees are replaced at a rate of two to every one harvested, some forms of forest management come under criticism from environmental groups. WEN believes that many of the natural old forests in the northern hemisphere have been replaced by cultivated trees grown as a crop with little regard for biodiversity and wildlife habitation. The process of converting wood to pulp demands vast amounts of energy and when chlorine is used to bleach the pulp, dioxins may be released into the environment.

NON-WOOD FIBRES

Non-wood fibre currently accounts for only 5 per cent of the total amount of fibre used in global paper manufacture, despite the fact that demand almost doubled in the 1980s. China is the largest producer, making over half the world's non-wood pulp. The most popular sources are straw, grown mainly in China and used in Eastern Europe, Pakistan and Turkey, as well as bagasse and bamboo grown in India. Esparto grass from Spain and North Africa is used in the production of stamp papers. Speciality papers such as those used for bank notes are made from cotton as well as ramie or Chinese grass, while Manila hemp or abaca is used in the making of cigarette papers and tea bags.

In Britain, the production of wheat and barley generates almost 10 million tonnes of agricultural waste in the form of straw which, according to WEN, if used in paper production could meet half the current demand. The paper industry has been investigating the potential of this raw material since the 1970s. However, as recent experiments carried out in Scotland and Denmark have experienced difficulties, it is widely agreed that more research is required.

Flax, traditionally grown throughout Europe for the production of oil, and linseed produce ideal fibres when pulped. Hemp, a strain of the cannabis plant containing very low levels of the drug found in marijuana, originates from Central Asia. In recent years it has become possible to obtain a licence for growing this crop and 800 hectares are now grown each year in Britain alone. The fibres derived from hemp are much longer than those from wood and so can be recycled more times. Due to its high yield, twice as much paper can be produced per hectare as from softwood grown in Northern Europe. At the Wookey Hole Mill in Somerset, the papermakers have developed a hand-made paper of unique texture made purely of hemp.

In the West, a renewed interest in the use of more diverse ingredients has encouraged us to look once again to the East and its abundance of unique papers born from local tradition and the use of indigenous plants. The growing Western market for hand-made plant fibre papers has helped to revive many practices in the developing world.

ACROSS THE WORLD

In Northern Thailand paper has been made from the bark of the *Thai-sa* or mulberry tree for centuries and used to make parasols, fans, kites and decorations for Buddhist temples.

Lokta, the traditional source of fibre in Nepal and Bhutan, is derived from the bark of the daphne tree. The pulp creates a thin, creamy coloured paper of extraordinary strength. When held to the light, its beautiful fibrous texture is revealed. Once made for Tibetan Buddhist manuscripts, it is now more widely used and exported to the West.

Jute, originally used in the manufacture of sacking, is grown in vast quantities in Bangladesh. Since the decline of this industry as a result of the introduction of more modern synthetic materials, it has been used for other purposes such as pulp for paper. In India, paper made from recycled jute sacking is called gunny paper.

In southern India, a wide choice of ingredients is employed in today's paper manufacture. Waste cotton or *khadi* is now the primary ingredient used in many of the papers which contain decorative additives such as tea, grasses, flower petals, and coloured silk or cotton threads, developed to interest the growing Western market. Other papers made from sources such as bagasse or sugar cane fibre, and banana leaf as well as rice straw and rice husks add to the expanding range now commercially available in the West.

Phragmites, a common river reed found growing on the edge of the dam of an old diamond mine in Kimberley, South Africa, is being used to beautiful effect, producing a fine quality, creamy coloured, hand-made paper with a crisp finish. A paper project initiated by Mara Amats provides work for some of the unemployed Tswana people from the local township of Greenpoint.

Right: The paper shown on the left is made with water hyacinth, a plant found in many Asian waterways. The paper on the right is made purely from denim offcuts, the original dye giving the sheet a soft blue, mottled effect.

Right: This selection of papers has an equally fascinating origin. At The Power Station Craft Centre in Botswana, elephant dung is being used as a source of fibre to make these papers with rich colours and textures.

Right: An assortment of papers originating from all corners of the globe, each made from a different plant fibre, giving it a distinctive texture and finish. Top right: envelope of English hemp paper; top half of photograph: Nepalese coloured lokta tissue; bottom half of photograph: Nepalese banana and lokta paper; right: two rolled sheets of Indian cotton paper with a rich mixture of coloured silk; bottom right: bag made of mulberry bark paper from Thailand containing Japanese textured silk tissue; bottom left: roll of fine calligraphy paper from China.

Virtually any plant with long fibres in its leaves or stems can be used for hand-made paper. Some non-wood fibres which contain more cellulose and less lignin than wood are an ideal substitute for traditional pulp. In the late eighteenth century, German naturalist Dr Jacob Christian Schaffer turned his attention to common plants such as potatoes, grape vines, tree moss, cabbage stalks, thistles and oak leaves as alternative sources of fibre for papermaking.

Denim or *Serge de Nimes*, translated as twill from Nimes, was originally invented during the nineteenth century in France and is most famous for being used by Levi Strauss to make practical and hard-wearing clothes for the miners of the California Gold Rush. The papermakers at the Wookey Hole Mill in Somerset have now developed an unusual paper made from denim offcuts imported from America. The original indigo dye is retained in the pulp, giving the paper its distinctive blue colour.

Water hyacinth, originally brought to Asia by a colonial British woman as a purely ornamental plant, has since run riot, clogging up many waterways right across the Asian continent. At the General Paper Industry's mill near Kathmandu in Nepal, papermakers have found a use for it, successfully pulping it and adding it to lokta fibre to create a unique fibrous paper with an interesting environmental story.

Southern Africa is not traditionally associated with papermaking. However, a rather intriguing raw material is now being utilised. The rhinoceros and elephant herds are contributing to paper manufacture as a new range of dung papers is being made in Botswana. The dung is floated on a surface of recycled pulp, giving the paper its unusual and unique texture.

THE QUESTION OF RECYCLING

The last decade has seen a surge in popular concern for the environment on a global scale. Recycling has begun to play a vital role in the pursuit of sustainability, but to the world of papermaking, this is not a new concept. The earliest record of recycled paper dates from fifteenth-century Japan where guilds of papermakers used reclaimed material from eleventh-century manuscripts from the Imperial Library. One of the oldest working mills in Britain, based at Frogmore Mill in Hertfordshire, has been making non-bleached, 100 per cent recycled paper exclusively since 1890 when the operation was taken over by The British Paper Company.

Each year 235 million tonnes of paper are disposed of worldwide, with approximately 85 million tonnes making up the recycled fibre used in global paper manufacture. Recycling in the paper industry makes not only commercial but also environmental sense.

RECYCLING IN THE WEST

In America, where the market for recycled materials is worth over $17 billion, 800 companies have pledged commitment to a scheme encouraging the purchase of recycled paper. In Britain, a similar programme named 'Buy Recycled' has been initiated by sectors of the paper industry and is aimed at companies, local authorities and the general public.

Surprisingly, there is no international agreed standard by which recycled paper is defined. In Britain, the ABCD scheme, a classification set up in 1990 by major paper suppliers, grades the paper by the type of recycled content. The National Association of Paper Merchants introduced a standard in the same year requiring that recycled paper contains a minimum of 75 per cent post-consumer waste.

The Blue Angel scheme in Germany goes further, qualifying recycled paper as containing 100 per cent waste, of which 51 per cent has to be low or medium grade waste. In order to qualify for the EC Ecolabel, a paper is judged by a complete 'cradle to grave' analysis which also takes into account the wider environmental impact of the manufacturing process. This encompasses water and energy consumption, the bleaching processes and treatment of effluent.

In the West, approximately 30 per cent of post-consumer waste paper is recovered, mainly from commercial sources such as the printing industry. This is reintroduced into the system and graded by hand. Top quality waste, comprising printers' offcuts and office paper, is used to make new recycled printing and writing paper. Medium quality printed papers, once de-inked, are used in the making of tissue and newsprint as well as some stationery. The lowest grade of material is recycled into papers and boards used for packaging.

The paper industry, however, would not survive without the use of some virgin pulp. It is estimated that paper fibres cannot be recycled more than four to six times before they are broken down too far and are no longer strong enough to be reintroduced into the system.

Not all paper can be recycled. Some papers contain what are known as 'pernicious contraries' or additives which render the paper unsuitable for recycling. These include plastics used for laminating, non-water soluble glues and latex. Certain greetings cards, envelopes, paper cups, nappies and wallpaper are all common articles which cannot be recycled. As technological advances result in the continual introduction of specialist papers designed with specific uses in the medical and food industries, environmental pressure groups such as Greenpeace argue that the manufacture of non-recyclable materials should be avoided altogether.

Across the world, as the retail and manufacturing sectors are being made more responsible for the disposal of the packaging they generate, we too have an individual responsibility to manage our waste. When we know that, in Europe alone, 30 per cent of the waste in our landfills is precious recyclable paper and board, recycling should play a larger part in everyday life.

WHAT YOU CAN DO

It is estimated that in the West the average household may throw away as much as 3 kg (7 lb) of packaging in a week. A quick glance into your waste bin will make you immediately aware of just how much of it is precious paper which could easily be recycled.

As individuals, we can effect change by considering how we manage the waste we ourselves generate. In our offices, factories, schools and colleges we can initiate and encourage paper collection schemes to save good quality paper which is ideally suited for recycling. In our homes we can divide our waste and recycle the paper and card packaging, newspapers and mailshots we usually discard. Ask yourself, 'Can it be used again?' before you throw away a sheet of paper.

Above: In the West only 30 per cent of waste paper is recovered from an estimated total of 235 million tonnes which is disposed of worldwide each year. At this recycling plant and collection point at San Juan del Rio in Mexico recycling is carried out on a vast scale.

Right: Apart from the enormous scale of machine paper manufacture, the main distinguishing factor is that it is made on a continuous roll. This paper-making machine is at the UK Paper Company's mill - New Thame Paper Company at Kemsley, near Sittingbourne, Kent.

FITNESS FOR PURPOSE

'Form follows function', a term widely used in various design professions, refers to the concept that the shape of an object should be pre-determined by its intended end use. The same is true of paper. The phrase 'fitness for purpose' is used in the paper industry when deciding whether a chosen paper has the necessary properties to fulfil a desired function.

There is a vast number of different machine-made papers, each developed with a particular purpose in mind. We take for granted the continual advances in the industry which, in turn, bring about change in the fields of science and medicine as well as the nature of manufacture, distribution and disposal of consumer goods. Many of us underestimate the research that goes into advances such as fruit juices and milk being packed and sold in watertight cartons, which are far lighter to transport than glass.

To quote just one example of this, a recent development in the paper industry may mean that in future our cereal cartons will no longer need additional packaging in the form of inner bags. It is hoped that a newly developed cardboard, lined with a translucent inner film to prevent moisture, air and micro-organisms from damaging the contents, will radically cut down on the present double packaging.

MACHINE-MADE PAPER

Mould-made paper, which emulates the qualities of hand-made paper, can be made by a cylinder mould machine. However, the mechanised process which results in machine-made paper produces a product of a different nature to hand-made, the most obvious distinguishing feature being that when made, it forms a continuous roll.

The basic process is the same. As the pulp and water mixture is spread onto a moving wire mesh, the fibres begin to bond together and the excess water is drained off by suction pumps. The continuous sheet is fed through large rollers to squeeze out the remaining water and then through heated cylinders which dry the paper before it is finally wound onto large reels.

The quality of machine-made paper is determined by its ingredients. Rags as a raw material, expensive both to buy and to process, are only used in the manufacture of the highest quality durable papers. Chemical wood pulp is produced by the chemical digestion of non-fibrous parts of the wood. Although of a high quality, the paper made is less durable than that made with rags. Mechanical wood pulp, which as the name suggests is a mechanical process involving the grinding down of logs, produces a larger quantity of pulp but of a noticeably lower quality.

Technological advances in the paper industry over the last fifty years have led to an abundance of commercially produced papers. These can be generally divided into two main categories: papers made for either printing or writing, and those made for packaging.

PRINTING AND WRITING PAPERS

Printing and writing papers are used in the production of glossy magazines, stationery, stamps, books, leaflets and posters, in fact all the conventional channels through which we communicate. This makes up the largest sector of the papermaking business.

Made from either chemical or mechanical wood pulp, these papers come in a wide variety of finishes. Coatings, such as china clay, may be applied to act as fillers, creating a smooth surface. Coated paper, or art paper, is used in the printing industry when high definition print quality is required. Depending on whether the coated paper is polished, a range of finishes can be achieved from high gloss, satin or matt.

A heavyweight paper is used for good quality brochures and publications while a lighter weight is used for printing magazines and catalogues. Airmail paper and cigarette papers are made from lightweight, uncoated papers whereas heavier uncoated papers are used for books, copier papers and writing paper. These are often 'sized', meaning rosin or alum is applied to make the surface less absorbent and thus more suitable to be printed and written on.

Standard business paper, often carrying a watermark, is available in two distinct textures. The terms 'laid' and 'wove' refer to the surface of the paper which is determined by the type of screen the paper is made on.

PACKAGING

On average, 40 per cent of all packaging is made from paper and board, producing paper bags, tubes, boxes, cartons and wrapping papers, 60 per cent of which is used in the food and drink industry. The role of packaging has increased significantly over the last 50 years, as we, the consumers, have become more accustomed to an ever-growing choice of goods. Although often criticised for not being environmentally sound, it is argued that without such packaging, more waste would be created as its main function is to protect the product from damage, contamination and pilfering. It also provides a surface upon which information about the product is presented.

Paper which is used for packaging food is classed as wrapping paper. There are many types, each with very different qualities dictated by the nature of the object to be wrapped. Greaseproof paper is made by wet-beating the fibres of wood pulp after they have been cooked and is primarily used in packaging greasy products. Butter and margarine are usually packed in vegetable parchment which is made by dipping unsized paper in sulphuric acid.

Different thicknesses of crepe paper are used for special packaging purposes where a stretchy quality is desired. The softened variety known as tissue is used for many personal and domestic applications. It is made by a process called 'creping' using a moist web.

Board is made in a very similar way to paper, the only difference being the thickness which is measured by weight per square metre. A paper is classified as a board when it is heavier than 220 gsm (grams per square metre) whereas, in comparison, a standard photocopier paper weighs 80 gsm.

Some boards are specifically made to be printed on and so are either coated on one side or laminated with a single sheet of printing paper. An example of this is white line chipboard which is made from waste paper and is used to pack a wide range of commercial goods. The next time you have breakfast, inspect your cereal carton and you will find that the printed side is white while the inside is grey. Ivory board, on the other hand, is of a higher quality and suitable for such applications as business cards. This is made up of a number of layers of high quality paper pasted together.

Leather pulp board is an expensive material made from scrap leather and waste vegetable fibre bound together with latex. This treatment makes it flexible and thus ideal in the production of caskets and shoes. Duplex boards are made up of two or more layers with each side being a different colour. Other heavier weight boards, such as hardboard and plasterboard, are used in the construction industry for lining, panelling and insulation.

SPECIALITY PAPERS

There are a number of diverse papers which do not fall into the categories already covered. These have very specific uses, for instance blotting paper, made from cut and beaten rags, giving it a bulky rough texture allowing it to absorb fluids rapidly.

Tracing papers are made in two different ways, one involving making the paper transparent by impregnating it with either oil or resin while the other, which is known as natural tracing paper, is heavily beaten to form a long-lasting surface resistant to erasure.

Carbon paper transfers ink onto a page below when written on. It is made simply by coating one side with carbon which is then bound with wax. Carbonless copy paper fulfils the same task without the use of carbon. It has a surface of tiny ink bubbles which burst when the pressure of a pen is applied to them.

Above: Machine-made papers are not only used for industrial purposes. In Chapter 3 you will find an abundance of machine-made papers used to stunning effect. This work, entitled 'Past' by Vibeke Bak Hansen, was inspired by a spiral fossil form, interpreted as a symbol of eternity. It was created with folded strips of paper.

Right: Kraft, meaning 'strength' in German, is manufactured from wood pulp. Due to its robust qualities, its main application is commercial packaging.

Right: Corrugated card is a common material with a beauty which is often overlooked. This versatile paper, most commonly used for box packaging, can be applied to a number of more interesting uses which capitalise on its unique strength and structure.

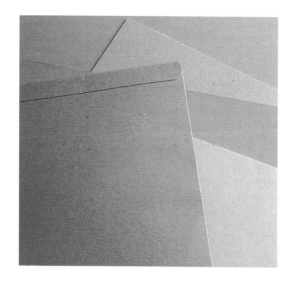

Right: Boards made using different processes with diverse applications. Lighter weights are used for packaging, bookbinding and stiffening envelopes. while heavier grades are moulded for use in car interiors and for the backs of television sets.

MACHINE-MADE PAPERS

Since the introduction of wood pulp paper and the first mechanical papermaking machines, an abundance of machine-made papers is now manufactured. These cover a vast range of options, varying in strength and texture, each designed with a particular purpose in mind. When viewed out of their usual context, the papers with their contrast of subtle tones and textures display a certain beauty in their simplicity.

Kraft paper comes in many colours, the most common being brown. Some are glazed on one side, some on both, while kraft union is made of two layers of paper laminated together to form a waterproof covering. It is used commercially and domestically for a variety of wrapping functions.

Corrugated papers make up about 56 per cent of all paper and board used for packaging. Generally taken for granted and serving the task of packing from the most fragile to the most mundane of products, when examined more closely, corrugated card has a particular beauty. It is available in a large variety of options, differing by number of laminated layers and width of the ribs, known as 'flutes'.

Millboard and fibreboard are heavy boards made of recycled vegetable fibres, and are used in unexpected industrial applications such as the insides of shoe heels and the backs of television sets. Fibreboard, the stronger of the two, is used in making items such as suitcases.

Right: A selection of machine-made papers, each manufactured with a specific purpose in mind. The varied assortment shown here includes, from top left to top right, decorative crepe paper, glasene, greaseproof paper, embossed wallpaper, newsprint; bottom left, patterned tissue; and bottom right, a selection of boards of different weights.

MAKING PAPER

'There is a trinity of three things that go into the making of paper that will last forever - materials, water, and the man who makes it.'

EISHIRO ABE *(the famous Japanese papermaker, designated a 'Living National Treasure' in 1968)*

This chapter is devoted to the activity of making paper by hand. Ideal for both beginners and more experienced papermakers, the processes are illustrated in three graded, step-by-step stages, using a wide range of fibre sources, from recycled waste paper to local plants. In addition, several variations to the basic papermaking techniques are included to inspire and encourage further experimentation.

Right: These fine examples of karakami papers dating back to the mid nineteenth century are from The Alcock Collection, held at the Victoria & Albert Museum in London. This form of Japanese wood block printing was used on kozo paper which was stretched over panels to make 'karakami-shoji' or decorated sliding panels for Japanese interiors. For more information on historic Japanese papers, see pages 12-13.

MAKING PAPER

In nineteenth-century Japan paper was made by farm workers during the winter months. Answerable to their feudal lords for the quality of their product, the papermaker would be punished severely, sometimes even to the extent of paying with his life, if his work did not reach the required standard. The papermakers strove for perfection, as quality rather than time was the issue, making the finest papers without a single speck or blemish.

The Japanese believe that every sheet of hand-made paper reflects the qualities of its maker. The craft is a highly individual activity which should be honoured with great esteem. Even though the process is essentially straightforward, it demands much practice and patience to reach a high level of proficiency.

In his book *Papermaking: The History and Technique of an Ancient Craft* (essential reference for all those interested in paper), Dard Hunter states, *'It is not possible to make really even sheets without at least five or six years of constant application at the vat...'*. He concludes, *'Unless one has a whole-hearted desire and enthusiasm to make paper by hand, one should never attempt it.'* You are invited to accept the challenge and join the many papermakers around the world who passionately devote their time to creating beautiful papers that are works of art in their own right.

Today there are two schools of thought amongst hand-made papermakers - those who believe that 'real' papermaking is for the purpose of providing a supreme printing and painting surface which can be recreated time after time, and those artists who experiment with many different fibres and textures to make papers of unique beauty with no other purpose in mind. Which philosophy you choose to believe and follow is up to you.

EQUIPMENT

A piece of paper can be made with simple equipment adapted from everyday household items, so for beginners wishing to try their hand at a new craft, an initial large expenditure can probably be avoided. However, for those who wish to embark on making paper or already practise the skill at a serious level, there are a number of tools worth investing in.

You may have to be resourceful to acquire specialist equipment. Despite the renewed interest in this craft, very few makers of papermaking tools still exist. It is possible to buy second-hand or laboratory equipment which is smaller and may be more suited to your needs, rather than larger, industrial-sized vats and beaters. In the list of suppliers on page 154 are some useful addresses and contacts to start you off on your quest. Alternatively, if you are technically minded or handy at DIY, you may be able to make some of the equipment or customise existing appliances and machinery to serve your needs.

The following list describes the essential tools required. Their uses are explained in the relevant step-by-step sequences to be found further on in this chapter.

MOULD AND DECKLE

A professional mould and deckle is made from mahogany with a bronze wire mesh and finished with copper and brass edging. These are still produced in limited numbers to the traditional specifications. Alternatively, contact suppliers of second-hand papermaking equipment and attend auctions to obtain older equipment. It is quite a thrill to own a mould and deckle from a prestigious mill, especially if it carries a watermark identifying either the mill or the papermaker. A simplified version of a mould and deckle can also be made by hand (see pages 36-37).

BLENDER

The process of blending can be carried out by a number of appliances - your choice depends on the amount of time you wish to spend making paper. If you plan to experiment on a small scale, a simple kitchen blender will be adequate. However, if you intend to produce large amounts of paper regularly, it may be worth investing in a more powerful beater. As preparing pulp is very time-consuming, a small Hollander beater, if you are lucky enough to acquire one, is designed specifically for the purpose and radically cuts down pulp production time.

VAT

Almost any waterproof container can serve as a vat, the size being determined by the dimensions of the mould. The important factor is that the mould and deckle must fit into the vat horizontally, with ample room either side for your hands. In the simple papermaking sequence shown on pages 38-41, a new cat litter tray is used as it is the ideal size for making A4 sheets.

PRESS

The simplest means of pressing paper is to use two boards which can be tightened together with carriage bolts. You may already own equipment such as flower presses or book presses which will serve the desired purpose, the only limitation being their size. It is also possible to adapt existing tools.

FELTS

In choosing materials to act as felts, there is an opportunity for you to improvise as almost any natural cloth can be used provided that it is strong and has a reasonably smooth surface. It is better to use a natural fibre such as haberdashery felt or even old woollen blankets because they are far better at absorbing the water. Professional felts are made from strong felted wool which is compressed into semi-rigid mats.

A WORD OF WARNING BEFORE YOU BEGIN

Some of the chemicals specified in the following step-by-step sequences are toxic and appropriate protective clothing must be worn when handling them. Before you begin, read the manufacturer's instructions carefully and use the products as intended. Avoid the use of chemicals where children are present.

Papermaking requires the use of liberal amounts of water and eletricity - a potentially hazardous combination. It is therefore important to make your working environment safe to avoid unnecessary risks.

Left: There are several pieces of basic equipment required for making paper by hand. The list includes a mould and deckle (centre), blender, vat, felts, a press (top), bucket and sieve. There is a wide range of raw ingredients to choose from, including waste paper, cotton linters and various plants.

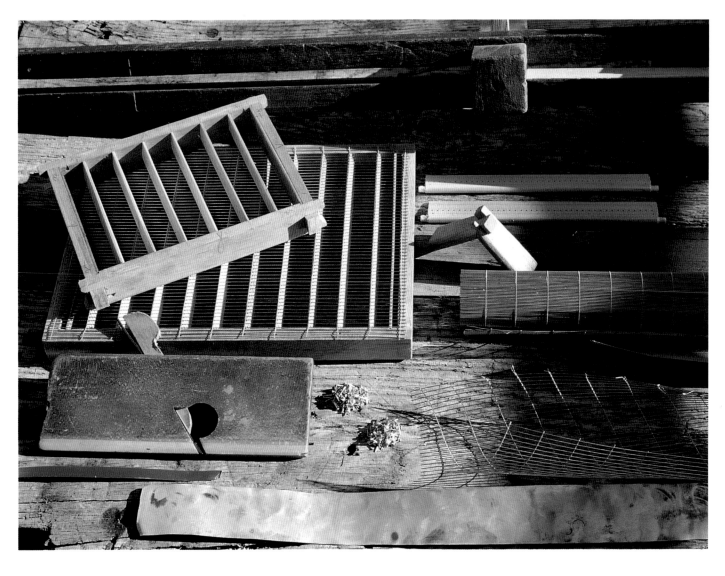

MOULD AND DECKLE

Above: Professional moulds and deckles made in the traditional manner require specially selected mahogany, copper and brass edgings with nails to match, and a choice of meshes woven with phosphor bronze wire. Also shown are some traditional specialised carpentry tools used to construct the moulds and deckles.

Moulds and deckles used by professional hand papermakers through the centuries are fine pieces of carpentry made by craftsmen using traditional methods. This once-common skill is now almost extinct, but Ron Macdonald, trained by his father after the Second World War, has continued his family tradition.

The main structure is made from specially selected mahogany, while the supporting bars are pine. The mesh which covers the mould (known as the 'face') is woven from phosphor bronze wire, a non-perishable metal, ideal for prolonged contact with water. There are two types of face to choose from, depending on the desired paper finish. A 'wove face' consists of a plain woven mesh which gives the sheet of paper a smooth texture. This weave varies between 12 and 70 holes per inch, the most common being 40 holes. It is speculated that the first woven mesh was commissioned by the typefounder and printer John Baskerville. Not satisfied with the commonly used laid moulds, he demanded a paper with a smoother finish.

A 'laid face' is a traditional weave, giving the paper a distinct, ribbed texture. The woven backing, a coarser laid weave, is sewn on to the bars of the mould, giving the face additional strength. It is possible to omit the backing on a laid mould if the papermaker wishes to enhance the laid texture of the finished paper.

Once the backing is sewn on and the chosen face attached to the mould, the top of the frame is finished with copper edging and fastened with copper nails. The deckle is made to fit over the mould and the corners finished with brass plates secured with brass nails. The bottom corners of the mould, which come into contact with the water when dipped in the vat, are finished with brass.

EQUIPMENT

Artist's wooden canvas
    stretchers (two sets),
    available from art
    supply shops
Fine wire mesh
Staple gun
Electrical insulation tape
Hammer
Scissors

MAKING A SIMPLE MOULD AND DECKLE

As with all processes, using the best tools for the job gives the best results. If you intend to make paper regularly and at a serious level, it is worth acquiring good quality tools. However, if you are experimenting with papermaking for the first time, it is possible to make a simplified version of a mould and deckle with which to make perfectly good sheets of a similar size.

Select a frame according to the desired size of your paper, bearing in mind that the finished sheet size will correspond to the inner measurements of the deckle.

Make up the two wooden canvas stretchers following the manufacturer's instructions, one to be used as a deckle and one as a mould. Measure a rectangle of wire mesh to fit over the mould frame, stretch it and tack it into place using a staple gun. Seal the top edge of the frame with lengths of electrical insulation tape.

A mould and deckle made in this way will be sufficient to experiment with. However, it will not be as satisfying to work with nor be as durable as the professional tools, so in time you may wish to invest in the real thing.

EQUIPMENT

Waste paper -
   approximately 50 sheets
   of A4 (210 x 297 mm/
   8⅓ x 11¾ in)
Bucket
Kitchen blender or
   liquidiser
Vat (or clean cat litter
   tray)
Mould (frame around
   which mesh is
   stretched)
Jug
Cloths and sponges

SIMPLE PAPERMAKING

The most basic method of papermaking is shown in the following step-by-step guide, demonstrating how to make a sheet of recycled paper on a mould. The floating of pulp on a screen resembles the earliest recorded process used by the Chinese, similar to the method still practised today in the Himalayan countries of Nepal and Bhutan. This method is extremely straightforward and therefore ideal for beginners.

The first stage is to collect together your equipment, most of which you will probably find around your home. It is important to use a suitable working environment with, above all, access to plenty of fresh running water and a spacious waterproof surface. As you may have imagined, papermaking is a messy activity involving large quantities of water so wear waterproof clothing or a large apron and protect your working area from accidental splashes by laying down old newspapers or other suitable coverings.

You will need to prepare the ingredients overnight, so read through the following instructions before you begin.

SELECTING THE INGREDIENTS

Begin by collecting waste paper which can be recycled. It is important to be selective as certain papers will not be suitable. Heavily coated and printed papers, such as glossy magazines and mailshots, are difficult to break down due to their coating and the dense layer of printed ink applied. Newspapers, although being an obvious choice for recycling, are also to be avoided due to their high acid content and very short fibres.

Another consideration is the type of ink used in printing newspapers which, unlike conventional printing ink, can be made up of industrial carbon waste and used engine oil. This will create an

1 PREPARING THE INGREDIENTS
Once you have chosen your papers and have collected a generous amount, tear them into small pieces measuring about 4 x 4 cm (1½ x 1½ in) - enough to half-fill a bucket. Pour in enough warm water to cover the paper pieces and leave overnight to allow the paper to become thoroughly soaked, ready for pulping the next day.

1

2 PREPARING THE PULP

Take a few handfuls of soaked paper from the bucket and place them into a shallow container with some water. Add enough water to make a porridge-consistency.

In the photograph here, a hand-held whisk is used to break down the fibres. Although a very effective tool, it must be used in short bursts to avoid burning out the motor. Alternatively, a kitchen blender will do the same job if you place a handful of soaked paper in the bowl and top it up with water to three-quarters full. Blend in short bursts until the pieces of paper have broken down, leaving a milky solution.

To test whether all the pieces have turned to pulp, pour some of the solution into a clear glass and give it a shake. If any solid pieces remain, the pulp is not yet ready and more blending is required.

2

3

3 PREPARING THE VAT

Fill the vat with clean water, then spoon or pour in a few batches of pulp following the general principle of one part pulp to four parts water. Agitate the water to disperse the fibres evenly.

The pulp is diluted in this way for better drainage through the mould face while the sheet is being formed.

unpleasant black scum on the surface of the water once the paper is soaked.

Suitable items to recycle include envelopes, notepaper, photocopier and tissue paper, all of which can be easily broken down, making them ideal for pulping. However, a sheet of paper made from these sources is likely to result in a dull grey colour.

If you wish to make a more durable sheet of recycled paper with a brighter tone, it is best to use plain hand-made or mould-made papers which can also be mixed with cotton linters. Available on a roll from specialist paper merchants (see suppliers on page 154), cotton linters are short fibres which cover the seeds of the plant, not used in the production of woven cotton. If you do not wish to spend a lot of time preparing pulp, cotton linters are ideal as they break down quickly and easily. Successful results can be achieved using cotton linters as the sole ingredient, making strong, white sheets of paper.

4

5

4 MAKING THE SHEET

To make the first sheet, hold the mould frame-side up over the vat. Collect some of the pulp and water mixture in a jug and pour it onto the surface of the mesh.

If you possess a more professional mould and deckle, you may wish to use the deckle to hold the pulp in place on the mould, as shown in the photograph here.

Repeat pouring until the whole mesh area is evenly covered with a layer of pulp approximately 1 cm (⅓ in) thick.

5 DRAINING THE MOULD

Position the mould on the side of the vat, allowing the excess water to drain through the mesh. If using a deckle, remove it once the water has drained away, ensuring that no drops of water land on the newly formed layer of fibres, so ruining the sheet.

6

6 DRYING THE SHEET

Stand the mould upright against a wall, preferably somewhere where the water can drain away. If you choose an outdoor location, avoid direct sunlight as this will cause the sheet to curl off the mesh. Leave to dry for about a day. By then, the fibres will have bonded to form a sheet of paper.

When removing the sheet, avoid tearing by rubbing the back of the mesh and teasing the paper off first at one corner before gradually peeling it away.

If you wish to press the sheet, place it under a board and heavy weight for a few days or use a book press.

See the paper directory on pages 60 and 61 for an example of the paper made here.

STORING PULP

If you possess a number of moulds, the sheet making process can be repeated until all the pulp has been used up. Once the sheets have been made, you may find a thin mixture of pulp remains in the water. Considering the time and hard work put into preparing the pulp, you may wish to save this for future use.

This is easily done by scooping the remaining pulp from the vat with a sieve and squeezing out the water by hand to create tight, little balls of damp pulp. These balls can be dried out in a warm place such as an airing cupboard, or stored in plastic bags while still damp and placed in the refrigerator for future use. The pulp will keep in the refrigerator for at least a week. If stored in the freezer, pulp may be kept for at least one month. When you wish to use it, simply dilute it into a vat of clean water and proceed as normal.

EQUIPMENT

Coloured waste paper -
    approximately 50 sheets
    of A4 (210 x 297 mm/
    8⅓ x 11¾ in)
Bucket
Blender (or Hollander
    beater as shown in the
    photographs)
Vat
Mould and deckle
Felts
Press
Sieve

TO ADD COLOUR AND
TEXTURE (optional -
see pages 48-49 for
instructions)
Crushed cinnamon sticks
    (one per sheet of paper)
Turmeric (approximately
    2 g/½ teaspoon per
    sheet)
Potpourri of dried flower
    petals

1

INTERMEDIATE PAPERMAKING

The following demonstration shows how to make paper using a mould and deckle, incorporating the process known as 'couching'. This involves transferring a layer of wet fibres from a mould face onto an absorbent surface known as a 'felt' in preparation for pressing. This is the most common papermaking method practised by Western hand-made paper mills throughout the centuries and it is still used today by both craftspeople and commercial papermakers.

This step-by-step guide shows an intermediate level of papermaking, as this method demands some skill and practise. Variations show how colours and extra ingredients such as turmeric, cinnamon and a dried potpourri of flowers and leaves can be added during the sheet-forming stages of the process to make papers with unique finishes and textures.

1 SELECTING AND PREPARING THE INGREDIENTS

There are many ways to introduce colour into the papermaking process, the most simple being the use of coloured material to produce the pulp. Here, yellow typing paper has been chosen which will result in a recycled paper of similar colour.

Prepare the ingredients for pulping in the same way as in the simple papermaking process, shown on page 38. Tear the paper into small pieces measuring about 4 x 4cm (1½ x 1½ in), and fill a bucket about half-full. Pour in sufficient warm water to cover the paper and leave overnight to allow the paper to become thoroughly soaked, ready for pulping.

2

PREPARING THE PULP
See Simple Paper-
making, page 39

2 PULPING

Half-fill the beater with
water. Pour in sufficient
soaked paper to achieve a
thick, soup consistency
and blend the mixture until
the paper breaks down to
a milky consistency.

Test the pulp in a clear
glass to check that no
solid particles remain (see
page 39).

3 AGITATING IN VAT

Fill the vat with clean
warm water and add the
pulp, at a ratio of one part
pulp to four parts water. It
is important to keep the
fibres suspended before
each sheet is made by
agitating the mixture or
'slurry'. This can be done
by hand or with a stick to
stop the fibres sinking to
the base of the vat.

3

4

4 DIPPING THE MOULD AND DECKLE IN THE VAT

Dampen the mould first with water. This will allow the water in the pulp to drain through the mesh more easily.

Holding the deckle by the frame close against the mould, lower them vertically into the far side of the vat, turning them towards you to a horizontal position as they become completely immersed in the pulp and water mixture.

5

5 PULLING THE FIRST SHEET

The primary function of the deckle is to contain the pulp on the mould when the mould and deckle are lifted out of the water together. However, it is inevitable that some stray fibres will penetrate under the deckle, giving the sheet what is known as a 'deckle edge'. This is the characteristic and distinguishing feature which is often left untrimmed and sets hand-made paper aside from neatly trimmed machine-made papers.

The fibres begin to gather on the mesh leaving a thick blanket of pulp. As soon as the water begins to drain away through the mesh, shake the mould and deckle in a forward-to-back and side-to-side, wave-like motion. This movement, known as the 'vatman's stroke', disperses the fibres in different directions, thus ensuring a good bonding action and a stronger resulting sheet.

6

6 DRAINING THE MOULD

Rest the mould and deckle on the side of the vat for about 30 seconds, allowing the excess water to drain away. The temperature of the vat mixture effects the speed of the drainage: the warmer the water, the faster it escapes. At this stage the sheet consists of approximately 90 per cent water.

To prevent water escaping over the sides of the vat while draining, use a long stick as shown in the photograph. Place it across the vat and rest one edge of the mould on it to allow the water to drain back into the slurry.

You will notice that as you continue to pull sheets, the consistency of the slurry will become thinner. When you are no longer able to collect enough fibres on the face of the mould to make a satisfactory sheet, replenish the slurry with some fresh pulp, once again agitating the mixture to disperse the fibres.

7

7 LIFTING OFF THE DECKLE

This manoeuvre requires attention as the deckle must be carefully lifted away from the mould, ensuring that no drops of water land on the layer of pulp as this could ruin the newly formed sheet.

If this does happen, turn the mould over and touch the surface of the water with the mesh, allowing the pulp to drop back into the solution. Agitate the mixture and prepare to pull another sheet.

8 PREPARING TO COUCH

The surface on which you couch your first sheet of paper should be made up of cloths known as 'felts'. If you do not own a professional set of felts, you can improvise by using old woollen blankets or thick, absorbent cloths. The felts must be larger in size than the sheets of paper being made and must be dampened with water before use.

It helps to lay some folded newspapers underneath the felt to make the surface slightly convex, thus providing a curved surface over which the mould will be rolled back and forth.

Prepare to couch the sheet by holding the mould vertically, with the layer of pulp facing away from you, and rest the bottom edge of the frame on the edge of the felt.

8

9

9 COUCHING THE SHEET

'Couching' refers to a method of transferring a layer of wet fibres onto a surface ready for pressing. To do this, lay the mould onto the felt face down and holding the frame, rock it back and forth a few times, gradually lifting it away to leave the sheet of fibres behind. Lay another felt over the freshly couched sheet, ready for the next.

It is important to interleave the sheets with felt to prevent the fibres of each paper bonding with one another.

When couching the next sheet, try to place it in exactly the same position as the previously couched sheet, building up an even layer. In commercial mills up to a hundred sheets would be couched onto a mound known as a 'post'.

Below: The function of a press is to expel the excess water from newly formed sheets as well as to press flat sheets of paper once they have been dried. A number of different tools can be used for this purpose, ranging from a simple flower press to a professional book press, as shown here.

10

11

10 PRESSING THE SHEET

Place the pile of felts and sheets in a press and apply considerable pressure for a few hours to expel the majority of the water. This action also assists in bonding the fibres together. With experience you will be able to estimate an appropriate length of time for your press to achieve the desired result.

If you do not own a press, you can improvise by placing the felts and sheets between two wooden boards and tightening them with carriage bolts.

11 DRYING THE SHEET

Once pressed, remove the post and gently peel each sheet away from its felt. This must be done with great care to avoid tearing the newly made sheet. Although the fibres in the sheet will have bonded together, the paper is still not strong enough to use, and must be allowed to dry out thoroughly.

Either lay the papers flat or hang them over a rope or railing, as shown in the photograph above.

Ideally papers should be dried in a gentle warmth. It is not advisable to expose the paper to too much heat as this may cause severe buckling of the sheets.

When completely dry, the paper will be slightly uneven and should be pressed once more in order to achieve a perfectly flat finished surface.

COLOUR AND TEXTURE

In ancient Japan the whiteness of a sheet of paper symbolised purity and is still used today to decorate Shinto shrines. However, in the West, some hand-made papers were traditionally coloured with a natural pigment resulting in a pale blue tint. The custom remains to this day, with the manufacture of classic writing papers in a choice of white or blue.

A larger choice of dyes is now available. Natural pigments derived from sources such as catechu (a resinous substance from the acacia tree), indigo and even onion skins can be used for subtle earthy tones. However, in order to extract the dyes and achieve the desired hues and colour fastness, chemicals must be added to act as mordants.

If you are not familiar with these complex dyes, begin with simple techniques involving readymade and easy-to-use colourings. For brightly coloured results, additives such as acid dyes, drawing inks and food colourings which are water soluble can be used. Experiment with ingredients such as turmeric and crushed cinnamon sticks for subtle tones.

An interesting array of elements can be added to pulp to make papers with unique textures and surface patterns. Coloured threads, fragments of mica (a silvery rock-forming mineral), feathers and dried petals are just a few suggestions.

Although there are no strict rules to follow, it is worth heeding a word of warning when using petals and plants. Ensure any plant material you select is dried before adding it to the pulp, as bleeding may occur when the sheet is pressed, resulting in unattractive stains. Even when dried thoroughly, some plants will cause this effect. Experiment with different materials to find an effect that you like.

There are two ways in which ingredients can be incorporated, either by being added to the vat and floated on the surface of the slurry, to be picked up on the mould with the pulp, or by being sprinkled onto the layer of fibres collected on the mould face.

1

2

1 ADDING INGREDIENTS TO THE VAT

Items can be floated in the vat ready to be picked up on the mould. Here a dried potpourri of plants and flowers is used, including rose petals, iris, lilies, carnations, mimosa, wheat, lichens, seed pods, bay leaves and clover.

2 ADDING INGREDIENTS TO THE MOULD

Another way of creating interest is to add elements on the mould while the sheet is being formed. Speed is of the essence, as the items must be applied quickly before the water drains away.

In the demonstration, crushed cinnamon is sprinkled onto the sheet which not only adds an attractive texture and colour to the paper but also a slight scent.

3 ADDING COLOUR TO THE VAT

There are three ways to add colour to the basic papermaking process.

Firstly, pulp can be dyed before it is diluted in the water-filled vat. Secondly, ingredients can be added directly to the vat. In the photo below, spice is used to colour the pulp. About

2 g (½ teaspoon) of turmeric is mixed into the slurry in a medium-sized vat to add a warm glow and interesting texture to a sheet formed from it. The third method is to dip a plain, dry sheet into a tray of dye before it is again dried and pressed.

If the basic pulp comes from a mixture of different sources such as recycled paper and cotton linters, the dyes may take to some fibres more strongly than to others, resulting in an intriguing mottled effect.

See pages 60 and 61 for examples of the papers made here.

ADVANCED PAPERMAKING

Making paper using plant fibres is considered by some hand papermakers as the pinnacle of achievement. This activity is labour-intensive, demanding both patience and skill, but the continual experimentation and quest for new textures and finishes reap many rewards. The choice of materials is abundant and often very inexpensive, affording the papermaker endless opportunities for self-expression.

Many common home-grown plants are a good source of fibre, including rhubarb, daffodil stalks, barley, corn, maize and onion skins. Refer back to Chapter 1 (pages 18-19) for more information on the various fibres traditionally used around the world and on new sources of fibre, from rhino and elephant dung to denim offcuts, currently being used to make paper.

Both beginners and more experienced papermakers are fascinated by the way plant fibre is transformed into pulp. Any material containing liberal amounts of fibre is an ideal ingredient for the production of pulp. Plant materials contain cellulose fibre, a carbohydrate which, when soaked in water, begins to decompose. The aim is to remove the fleshy substance, made up of the sulphur compounds and sugars which hold the fibres together, from the plant material. This is done by a heat process which involves boiling the matter in caustic soda or soda ash. The remaining fibres are separated further into individual filaments by crushing and macerating.

In Japan, about 70 per cent of the total production time in the making of paper is traditionally devoted to the preparation of ingredients, so follow their lead and prepare the fibres properly to ensure a perfect finished result.

THE RAW MATERIAL

In choosing ingredients for your papermaking, be imaginative and resourceful as many home-grown plants create unique results (refer to Chapter 1 for information on suitable plants and fibres).

Here the fibre used is from the phragmites plant, a large river reed which grows in wetland areas. The largest growing area in England is at Walberswick, a marsh on the Suffolk coast managed by English Nature, a government-run conservation group. As part of the wildlife management, the phragmytes plants are cut back throughout the year to make room for other rare marshland plants. The cut reed is sorted into bundles, reserving the larger stalks for thatching. About 20,000 bundles a year come from this area alone and the by-product is used by local papermaker Mara Amats.

EQUIPMENT

Phragmytes (a large
   quantity as they shrink
   to one-tenth of their
   original volume when
   broken down)
Shredder or large scissors
Container to boil in (must
   be either enamel or
   stainless steel)
Caustic soda or other
   alkali, such as soda ash
Bleach (optional)
Hollander beater or other
   blending tool
pH testing papers
   (optional)
Vat
Mould and deckle
Felts
Press

Left: Phragmytes, a species of river reed, is an ideal ingredient for making paper. Here it is shown in various forms, from its dried state (once it has been shredded), then soaked and finally bleached, ready to be added to the blender and made into pulp.

1

2

1 SHREDDING

Cut the chosen plant material into small, manageable pieces.

If you are making a small amount of paper for experimentation, this can be done simply by cutting it with a pair of scissors. If larger amounts are needed, a garden shredder, as shown in the photo, is ideal for the job.

It is important to remember that a lot of plant material does not go a long way. Once the plant matter has undergone the processes of soaking, boiling, beating and pulping, it will shrink to about one-tenth of its original bulk.

2 SOAKING AND BOILING

This step is crucial in the papermaking process and greatly affects the quality of the finished sheet. The object is to remove the fleshy part of the plant from the cellulose fibres.

First, soak the plant matter in water to begin decomposition. It can be left soaking for up to a month by which time it begins to give off unpleasant odours. Although a shorter period is adequate, the longer you soak the plant material, the easier it is to work with as the water breaks down the fibres.

Next, boil the matter, adding caustic soda to the water. As a guide, use about 3 tablespoons per large cooking pot. Boil for 1½-2½ hours to break down the unwanted substances. Use a large enamel or stainless steel container. Do not use an aluminium vessel as it will give off dangerous fumes when filled with boiling caustic soda. Once boiled, it is vital to rinse the plant matter properly in fresh water to remove any residual chemicals.

At this stage you may wish to bleach the matter to alter the colour of your finished sheet. This is done by soaking it in a solution of water and household bleach; the length of time depends on how pale you wish to make the pulp. All the bleach must be diligently rinsed out to ensure the plant matter is absolutely clean. It is important to note that although vital to the process, chemicals do weaken the fibres and so the larger the quantity the more damage caused.

3 BLENDING

In many papermaking regions around the world, the ingredients are beaten by hand for many hours to break down the fibres. This extremely labour-intensive activity can now be done with the help of a beater. The Hollander beater is the standard industrial tool, designed specifically for making pulp for paper production.

If you own a small beater, add the plant material to the beater, filled with water. Blend for between 20 minutes and

3

1½ hours, depending on the quantity and consistency of the fibres and the desired finished effect. Alternatively, a powerful kitchen blender is adequate if used in short bursts to avoid burning out the motor.

If you are concerned about the durability of your paper, which can be affected by the acidity of

the pulp, aim for a neutral pH value of 7. Using standard testing papers, the pulp can be tested at any stage of the process to ensure the correct balance is maintained.

Make the sheet by following the steps on pages 44-47 by preparing the vat, dipping the mould and deckle, couching, pressing and drying.

See the paper directory on pages 60 and 61 for an example of the paper made in this particular demonstration.

DIPPING THE MOULD AND DECKLE IN THE VAT
See Intermediate Papermaking, page 44

COUCHING THE SHEET
See Intermediate Papermaking, page 46

EMBEDDING

Embedding is a technique by which a decorative element can be encased within the fibres of a sheet of paper. This is done by placing a chosen ingredient which is very light and two-dimensional on the mould face as the sheet is being formed. As the paper dries, the added detail is suspended inside the sheet.

The earliest recorded form of embedding dates back to ancient Japan where papermakers would add plant life, threads and gold and silver leaf to papers, sometimes even strands of their own hair to identify their sheets. More recently, at the Nawa Museum of Entomology in Gifu, Japan, butterflies and insects have been embedded in paper.

In the photographic sequence shown here, a dried fern leaf is embedded into a sheet of recycled paper. Experiment with other items, such as birds' feathers and stamps, to personalise your paper. Begin by following the step-by-step guide on the previous pages on making paper using a mould and deckle, either the intermediate technique showing how to make recycled paper or the advanced technique illustrating how to make paper using plant fibres. Start by practising the technique using a heavy weight of hand-made paper as the more pulp there is to work with, the easier it is for your object to become successfully embedded. For more information on working with dried flowers and plants, refer to the section on adding colour and texture on page 48.

1

2

EQUIPMENT

Vat of pulp and water
 mixture
Mould and deckle
Dried fern leaf

1 EMBEDDING

This very simple procedure demands speed to achieve a successful result, as it is employed just at the point where the sheet of paper is being formed. When lifting the mould and deckle out of the water, carefully lay the dried fern on the surface of the pulp, before the water begins to drain away. The fern will become embedded within the fibres of the sheet.

For the most effective results, select items which are lightweight and flat so that the fibres partially cover the object, ensuring that it is held in place once the sheet is couched. Continue in the usual way to finish the sheet (see pages 40-41)

SIZING

The term 'waterleaf' refers to a sheet of paper before 'sizing', a treatment which renders the sheet less absorbent and more suited to receiving writing and printing inks as well as paints. The ingredients and methods of application have varied over time and across continents.

In traditional Oriental papermaking, a vegetable mucilage commonly known as *neri* was added to the pulp mixture in the vat before the sheets were formed. This slowed down the drainage through the screen, enabling the papermaker to form an even sheet which was both extremely thin and very strong. Miraculously, this solution allowed the sheets to be couched on top of one another without the need for interleaving and, even after pressing, the sheets could be easily peeled apart. This process, first used in around AD 700, is still employed by papermakers across the world who use the Oriental method.

By the eleventh century, Arabs were washing boiled rice to obtain rice starch and mixing it with an equal quantity of chalk to add whiteness. The papers were coated and once dry, polished with a glass burnisher. By the fourteenth century, animal glue was used in the mills of Europe. Starch, gelatin, animal glue and synthetic resins are all used in papermaking today.

If you intend to write, paint or print on your hand-made paper, you are advised to follow the centuries' old tradition and size it first. If you apply ink or paint to unsized paper, it will act in a similar way to blotting paper and absorb the liquid into the fibres, causing a bleeding and feathering effect. Paper can be sized using a number of methods, one being to soak the dry sheet in a solution of size and water before it is finally dried and pressed flat. Two other methods are explained on this page.

1

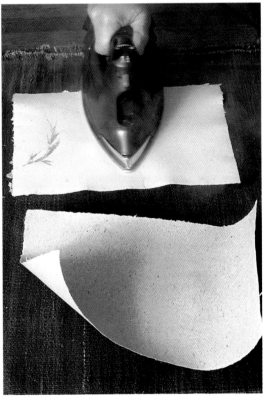

2

1 ADDING SIZE TO THE VAT

The size can be added directly to the vat mixture. In this photo methyl cellulose powder is used at a quantity of half a cup to a small sized vat. This is thoroughly mixed into the pulp and water before the sheets are made. (The powder is available from art suppliers.)

2 ADDING SIZE TO THE PAPER

Starch is also available in spray form. Apply the starch liberally to a dry sheet of paper, and immediately run a hot iron over the sheet. This gives the surface an attractive sheen, simultaneously flattening the paper. If you wish to have the same finish on both sides, repeat the treatment on the reverse.

Right: The original masterplate and cast used to produce the watermarks for a series of historic British stamps.

WATERMARKS

The term 'watermark' refers to an image placed in a sheet of paper during the making process that is visible in its full glory when the dried sheet is held up to light. It is created by raised areas on the surface of a mould face where the paper fibres collect in a thinner layer.

The origin of watermarks, as with much of the history of papermaking, is rather unclear. It is agreed that the first watermarked papers appeared in the thirteenth-century in Italy and became popular throughout Europe during the fifteenth century. The traditional watermarked papers depicted symbols of fruits, animals and simple shapes such as crosses and circles. Some early watermarks identified paper mills and even individual papermakers.

Throughout history, watermarks have played an essential role in both the prevention and detection of forgeries, and have been used as important evidence in many famous court cases. The Bank of England used increasingly elaborate types of watermark in the battle against counterfeiters which raged at the turn of the nineteenth century. In an attempt to discourage the hundreds of forgers operating at the time, Sir William Congreve tried, unfortunately without success, to persuade the Bank of England to introduce his unique papermaking invention, the 'triple paper', which displayed the first coloured watermark.

At the same time, another invention, the 'chiaroscuro' or embossed watermark, elevated the craft into a league of its own. Used in France and England, this advance allowed elaborate and complex images to be reproduced with all the detail of a photograph. An image, often a portrait, would be intricately carved in a wax tablet and male and female (i.e. opposing) moulds cast from it. The cast mould would be used to compress the image into a

Above: A fine example of an antique embossed mould face. The paper made from this mould would depict a watermarked image with subtle details of light and shadow.

wove face which was then attached to a papermaker's mould. Great skill and a specially prepared pulp of very short fibres were required to reproduce a faithful copy of the original image in a sheet of paper.

Today, watermarks are very common, especially in all types of stationery products. However, like so many of the traditional papermaking processes, the technique has now become more mechanised. Images are built up with the use of electrolysis and placed in position on enormous industrial rollers called dandy rolls. These are fixed to the papermaking machine, impressing the watermarks in the wet layer of fibres as the paper is made. It is possible to commission a special run of paper bearing a watermark if a large quantity is ordered. This service is offered by a number of international paper manufacturers.

If you wish to personalise your hand-made paper with a watermark, you will find that the traditional hand-sewn method is surprisingly straightforward. There are still some commercial watermark makers who take on individual commissions operating today, such as Ron Macdonald of Edwin Amies and Son, located in Maidstone, England. The step-by-step demonstration on the following pages shows the process of applying a simple wire-frame watermark to a mould face.

Where a single watermark is to be repeated a number of times on a sheet, a masterplate is made. The original wire frame is repeatedly pressed into a tablet of wax the required number of times and an electrotype is then made by the process of electrolysis. Identical wire frame images are cast from this mould, which is known as the masterplate. This method is used for creating watermarks in stamps, as shown by the masterplate for a series of stamps (pictured on page 56), produced by Edwin Amies and Son, for the Royal Mail in Britain.

EQUIPMENT

Motif for watermark drawn on paper
Fuse wire (copper wire coated in tin for soldering purposes)
Pliers
Weights to hold wire in place during tracing
Scissors, for cutting the wire
Wove mould and deckle
Phosphor bronze wire (36 gauge)
Needle or pin tong

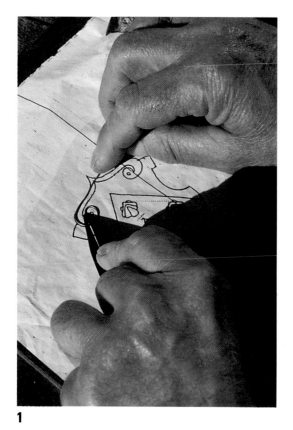

1

2

1 TRACE THE TEMPLATE WITH WIRE

Draw a template of your chosen motif to size on a sheet of paper. The motif should be drawn as a diagram and made up of open spaces, so that when paper is formed on the mould, the pulp does not clog.

Remember that the watermark is created by a thinner layer of fibres, so do not include solid areas as these will create holes in the paper. Also avoid sharp angles as they are hard to achieve. Dots pose a problem as they cannot be sewn into the wire mesh; replace these with circles.

Bend the fuse wire with pliers, following the contours on the template. Hold the wire down on the paper with weights.

The gauge of the fuse wire depends on the thickness of the paper to be made, for instance a heavyweight paper such as blotting paper would require a watermark made of 18 gauge wire, whereas a finer paper would require 26 gauge. The tin coating on a fuse wire is for ease of soldering.

2 SEW THE WIRE FRAME ONTO THE MOULD

Once the wire frame is complete, it is sewn onto the face of the mould with a needle and fine phosphor bronze wire. The image may be made up in sections and soldered together to form a single wire frame, or sewn directly onto the mould, section by section.

When using a laid face, it is correct to position the motif centrally between two vertical laid lines. Watermarks which incorporate lettering should be sewn onto the face reading back to front, as the right side of a sheet is traditionally the one in contact with the mould face when the paper is made. This applies to papermaking in Britain and North America; however, in France the reverse is true.

3

3 PREPARE FOR MAKING THE PAPER

The mould is now ready for making paper with the added value and decorative appeal of a personalised watermark.

Follow the instructions for intermediate or advanced papermaking earlier in this chapter (pages 42-53).

Above: Shown here is the final wire frame secured on a wove mould face. The raised areas on the face cause the fibres of the newly formed sheet to collect in a thinner layer, creating a shadow of the image, seen in its full glory when the paper is held up to the light.

Left: This sheet, by Jim Patterson of The Two Rivers Paper Company, was made from the watermarked mould shown above.

Right: The background sheet of recycled paper was made during the simple papermaking process on pages 38-41. The yellow sheet on the left was made during the intermediate process on pages 42-47.

Right: These papers, made from pulp derived from a river reed known as phragmytes, were made during the demonstration of advanced papermaking on pages 50-53. The sheet on the left is made from bleached pulp, while pulp in its natural colour was used to make the sheet on the right.

Right: This selection of beautiful hand-made papers was made during the demonstration of intermediate papermaking on pages 42-49 where interesting variations were added to the basic process to create subtle textures and colour. From top right to bottom left: paper made with coloured recycled paper pulp with crushed cinnamon and a sprinkling of turmeric; plain recycled paper pulp with crushed cinnamon and turmeric; plain recycled paper pulp with cinnamon; coloured recycled paper pulp and turmeric; and in the background, paper made with plain recycled paper pulp with an added potpourri of dried plants and flowers.

HAND-MADE PAPERS

In this chapter we have described the various methods of making paper by hand. This directory displays actual examples of all the papers made during these demonstrations.

The technique of simple papermaking shown on pages 38-41 involves the preparation of a pulp made from recycled paper. The sheet is formed simply by pouring the diluted pulp onto the face of the mould, allowing the excess water to drain. The fibres are left to dry on the mesh, and the paper is then gently peeled away and pressed.

The technique of making paper using a mould and deckle is shown in intermediate papermaking on pages 42-49. This method incorporates the process of couching, whereby a layer of wet fibres is transferred from the mould face onto a surface known as a felt before it is pressed and dried. The raw material used here is coloured typing paper, resulting in an evenly coloured sheet. A number of variations are explored to achieve additional colour and texture. Spices are used to enhance the tones and surface finishes, while ingredients (in this case a dried potpourri of flowers and plants) are added to the fibres to personalise the paper.

The technique involving the use of plant fibres as the primary ingredient for pulp is shown in advanced papermaking on pages 50-53. Although the basic process of forming the sheet resembles the intermediate method, the preparation of the pulp requires more time and effort. The raw material used is phragmytes, a species of river reed. It has been used in its natural form, resulting in a rich, dark cream sheet. The same pulp is also bleached, giving the paper a paler tone. A large number of common plants may be used to form pulp. For more information refer to pages 18-21.

PAPER TECHNIQUES

'Paper was purity itself in Shinto worship;
it marked the enclosure of sacred areas and
signified the living presence of the gods.
Paper was at once the most cherished of
substances and the most disposable.'

SUKEY HUGHES - *Washi*

In this chapter, we turn our attention to the many
ways that paper can be used. Using hand-made
and contrasting machine-made papers, a wide
variety of techniques and applications are
demonstrated. These are divided into three
categories - using paper as a raw material,
applying a variety of surface decorations, and
transforming paper into three dimensions.

WORKING WITH THE RAW MATERIAL

A sheet of plain paper is often regarded in the same way as a blank canvas, valued only when it carries an image or printed word. However, when treated as a raw material, paper can afford us myriad opportunities, lending itself to an inexhaustible list of treatments due to its unique composition. It can be transformed into a fresh and unique material or object when torn, cut, punched, stamped, pierced, folded, pleated, woven or crumpled. The following techniques illustrate how paper can be manipulated in a seemingly infinite number of ways to create a diverse array of effects and finishes.

We begin this chapter with an introduction to creating decorative markings. This demonstration draws on techniques adapted from other crafts, as in the case of repoussé or the punching of metal. The demonstrations of crumpling, folding, pleating and weaving draw on the traditions of ancient Japan where paper, for centuries the primary raw material, was used with ingenuity and resourcefulness.

Previous page: Ann Frith works with papier mâché to decorate her unique furniture pieces, using layers of paper pulp to emphasise the fluid, undulating shapes.

CREATING DECORATIVE MARKINGS

'Repoussé' is the name given to the art of manipulating metal to create decorative markings. The material is quite literally pressed, scored and punched on the reverse, revealing a relief pattern on the correct side. Common materials used for this technique are soft metals such as tin, copper and aluminium. This is a popular craft in Mexico, India and the Philippines, where the process is often semi-mechanised with the use of stamping tools.

In the demonstration shown here, the technique has been successfully applied to foil-coated papers, creating the illusion of metallic surfaces. Almost any paper of sufficient weight and strength will be equally effective. The following step-by-step guide shows a range of simple patterns, created with a choice of implements, each with its own characteristic marking.

Left: The surface of a sheet of paper can be manipulated in a number of ways to create decorative markings. These foil-coated papers provide an effective surface on which to display the many varied effects which can be achieved with common instruments and tools, as shown by Deborah Schneebeli Morrell in the following demonstration.

EQUIPMENT

Range of coloured foil
    papers
Hole punch
Letter and number
    punches
Hammer
Haberdashery tracing
    wheels
Bradawl
Paint brush
Newspaper, to protect
    the worksurface

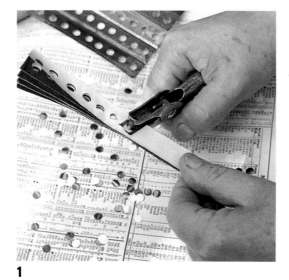

1

2

1 PUNCHING

With the use of a
stationery hole punch,
multiple holes may be cut
out of the paper, either in
a set pattern or at random.

The technique
illustrated here shows the
paper being folded into a
fine concertina measuring
no more than 2 cm (¾ in)
wide and holes being
punched along its length.

When unfolded, the paper
takes on a quality of
industrial geometry, and
looks very effective with
light shining through.

2 STAMPING

Many individual stamping
tools are available from
tool shops and makers.
These include letters of
the alphabet or numbers
and decorative symbols,
such as stars.

Lay the foil paper face
down on a thick pad of
newspaper paper to
protect your worksurface.
Place the chosen symbol
face down on the reverse
of the paper, then hit the
stamp with a hammer to
impress the symbol into
the paper.

The image will appear
embossed on the correct
side of the paper. Using
various symbols, repeat
this action to create a
pattern of your choice.

3

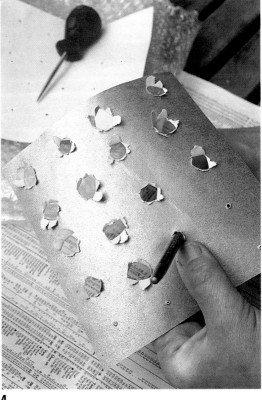

4

3 ROLLING

Haberdashery tracing wheels are commonly used to trace dressmaking patterns onto pattern paper to make templates for garment making. The tool leaves a distinctive pierced marking of spaced pin holes and can be rolled over the paper in straight or curved lines, as the pattern dictates.

Here, the wheel has been used to great effect by running it over the reverse side of foiled papers, creating a gently embossed pattern on the metallic surface.

As with the stamping, protect the worksurface with a pad of old newspaper. A variety of markings can be achieved with a choice of wheels, so look in haberdashers or department stores for different wheels.

4 PIERCING

Lay the paper reverse side up on a soft surface, such as a bundle of bubble wrap or newspaper, and repeatedly pierce it in a chosen pattern with a bradawl.

Widen each individual piercing with the end of a paint brush. Push the brush through the hole from the reverse side of the paper to the widest point of the handle, tearing the paper as you go. This action will leave holes with paper torn round the edges which can be folded back on the correct side. In this way, the resulting pattern is transformed from rather rough, bullet hole-shaped piercings to resemble flower petals.

PAPER AND LIGHT

ABOVE

The distinctive wall light shown here is designed and made by Joanne McCrum of Off The Wall Lighting. This sunflower shade is created in recycled paper treated with a flame retardant. Once the sheet has been curved over the wall fitting, rays of light shine through to illuminate the decorative detail cut in the paper.

RIGHT

Tomoko Azumi, a Japanese designer based in England, uses paper to create her unique pieces of furniture and lighting. This paper lamp, entitled *Trophy*, is made from two contrasting materials, paper and steel. The stainless steel rods are placed between layers of wet paper made of recycled egg packaging, jute and Japanese paper. The shape of the piece is formed by the natural process of the paper shrinking over the rigid frame and is back lit.

BELOW
Danish artist Anne Vilsbøll, internationally renowned for her work with paper, decorated the six glass sliding doors of the Danish Church Skæring. This door is adorned with coloured and natural hand-made daphne fibre paper, torn into small pieces and glued onto the glass.

RIGHT
This intriguing piece by Danish artist Mette Grue-Sørensen is a floor lamp entitled *Royal Campfire*. The design is an abstract spiral giving an unusual and dramatic light caused by the low placement of the bulb, throwing a web-like shadow. It is constructed from hand-made Thai kozo and abaca paper, which is cast together with fibreglass to stiffen the paper and give it a shiny waterproof surface.

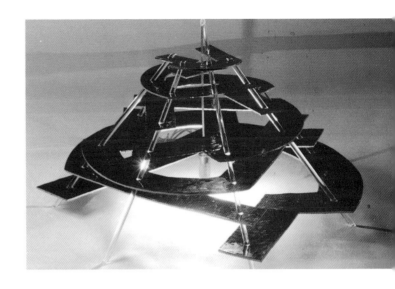

FOLDING AND PLEATING

Pleating is both a decorative and functional technique applied to a wide variety of materials for many different purposes. For example, in the case of an accordion or bellows, it allows a material to be repeatedly condensed and then stretched. With fabric it adds volume and provides warmth when used in curtaining and clothing. It makes it possible for a surface to be condensed into a smaller space, as in the case of a gusset on a paper bag or the walls of a briefcase. It also increases the structural strength of a material as illustrated by corrugated plastic or iron sheeting.

Paper is an ideal material for pleating as it retains creases and its flexibility allows the folds to be opened and closed. In this sequence, a diamond-shaped pleat is applied to paper and folded, creating a flexible surface of unique beauty. This technique can be used on a wide variety of papers, provided that the weight is not less than 100 gsm. A coloured, embossed 150 gsm paper has been chosen for this demonstration.

Left: Paper can be folded into intricate pleats, allowing a flat surface to become flexible and functional. This ingenious diamond-shaped pleat made by Andrew Bennett is made into a cylinder shape, creating a box which can be extended or flattened.

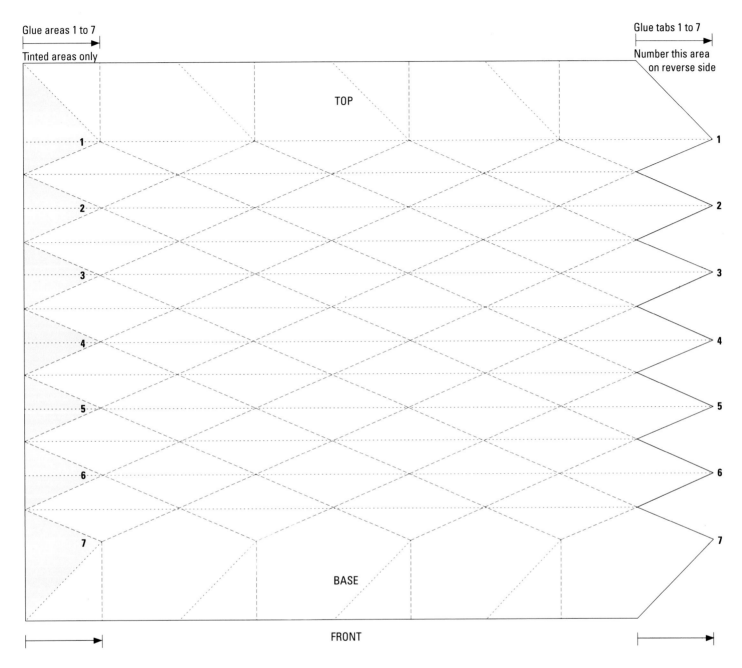

Glue areas 1 to 7

Tinted areas only

Glue tabs 1 to 7

Number this area
on reverse side

TOP

BASE

FRONT

CREATING THE TEMPLATE

Photocopy the template shown here onto an A3 sheet of paper (this template is shown in a reduced form, so you will need to enlarge it to 200 per cent on the copier).

Redraw or trace the grid very accurately onto the reverse side of your chosen sheet of paper. If you have access to a light source (such as a light box), this is the easiest way to do this.

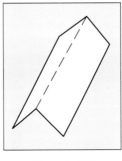

Mountain Fold

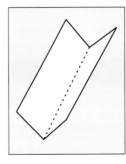

Valley Fold

The fold shown on the left is referred to as a 'mountain fold', meaning that it is raised, while the 'valley fold' shown on the right is indented.

EQUIPMENT

150 gsm paper, A3 size
(297 x 420 mm/11 ¾ x
16 ½ in)

Pencil

Metal ruler

Scalpel or scissors

Blunt knife, letter opener
or hard pencil

Glue stick

1 CREASING AND MAKING THE FOLDS

The action of creasing leaves an indent in the paper where the fibres are weakened, making it easier to fold. This is done by pressing down hard with the blunt side of a scalpel blade, letter opener or a hard pencil. Take care not to cut the paper. Run your chosen tool along all the lines on the template, using a ruler to ensure accurate and straight lines.

Carefully trim along the outer cut line using scissors or a scalpel and metal ruler. Then mark the top and bottom of the box and number the tabs down each side, as shown on the template on the previous page.

Fold the diagonal crease lines on the reverse side of the paper by placing a ruler by each line and bringing the paper up against the ruler. Repeat until all the lines are folded and finish by smoothing down each fold with the flat edge of a blunt knife.

Turn the page over and fold the horizontal lines in the same way.

1

2 COLLAPSING THE FOLDS

By holding both the outer edges of the creased and folded sheet, gently ease it into the shape of a cylinder. The pleats begin to collapse, the diagonal creases appearing as mountain folds (i.e. raised), while the horizontal creases become indented, thus creating valley folds. Take care that the folds do not invert the wrong way.

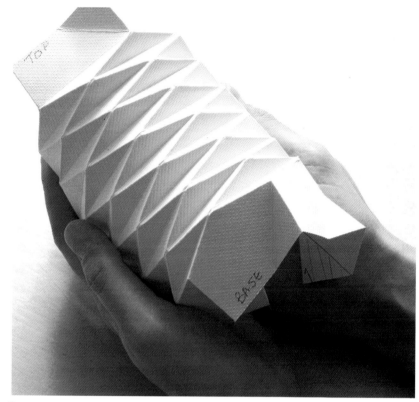

2

3

3 MAKING THE BOX

Turn the cylinder so that the cut edges and glue tabs are facing upwards. Apply glue neatly to tab 1 and fix to the tinted area 1, then apply glue to tab 7 and fix to the tinted area 7. As the box is under tension, the sides tend to spring open so make sure the glue tabs 1 and 7 are secured in place while the cylinder dries.

Fold down the top and base so they are flat. Apply glue to tabs 2-6 and bring into position. Bring the top and base together as shown to collapse the pleats until flat. Draw the edge of the kitchen knife firmly over each tab to fit it permanently to its glue position and leave to dry.

Open the top and base and hold the box through the open top with the base of the box facing up. Work round each of the fold lines in the open base, inverting each one as you go. This should bring the excess paper to the inside of the box and flatten the base. Fold down the top. The box is now ready to use as a piece of gift packaging or as a useful container.

PLIABLE PAPER

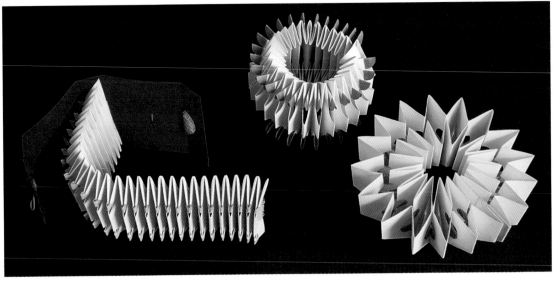

ABOVE

The Japanese designer Reiko Wanibuchi produces intricate paper folds and pleats to create a range of functional objects with defined geometric forms. The examples shown here are constructed using coloured paper, coloured elastic and wooden beads and include a concertina notebook, a pop-up folded paper bracelet with a velcro catch and a collapsible folded paper bracelet.

LEFT AND BELOW

Artist Nel Linssen uses paper to create sculptural pieces by cutting sheets into simple shapes and then gluing and twisting the structures to achieve forms which are beautiful in their simplicity. The unusual necklace shown below is made of folded paper circular shapes. The two piles are turned on an elastic tube to create this exquisite twisted form. The collection of three bracelets pictured on the far left is constructed from rectangular pieces of coloured, coated paper which have been glued in place.

ABOVE

These unusual paper envelopes by Mary Butcher are made of hand-woven white writing paper. The subtle abstract surface decoration is created by the chosen raw material, in this case the artist's own recycled hand-written notes and personal letters. These are cut into fine strips and woven using a bias plaiting technique, personalising the envelopes with part of the artist's life story.

RIGHT

American artist Mary Ann Lomonaco combines her own paper made from 100 per cent cotton cloth and abaca with 30 mm (⅛ in) painted wooden dowels, cold water dyes and linen yarn to create this stunning piece entitled *Iris*. The paper is couched onto a vacuum table and wooden dowels placed between the wet sheets of pulp before the vacuum process begins. Thirteen sheets are attached at regular intervals on each side using linen yarn. Each stack of attached sheets is sewn to a lucite form which hooks onto two screws in a wall. This causes the stack to hang out in a curve, like a butterfly's wings.

WEAVING

The practice of weaving with paper dates back to seventeenth century Japan where a technique known as *shifu* was developed. Hand-made paper or *washi* was sliced into fine strips, twisted into continuous threads and woven into a fine cloth. *Shifu-gami*, the paper created specifically for this purpose, was made in such a way that the fibres lay along the sheet, making it especially strong across the width. The finest quality *shifu* was woven with a silk warp, although the most commonly used warp was cotton. A *shifu* woven with both a warp and a weft of paper yarn was most commonly used by the lower classes.

This versatile and ingenious material, renowned for its strength, had a wide range of uses, from footwear, bags and purses to clothing and even army uniforms. Nobumitsu Katakura is credited with having revived this ancient craft after the Second World War and today it is practised in Japan by a handful of weavers.

In the West, a paper yarn or tape is used in the mass production of lampshades and mats. In the demonstration shown here, machine-made paper yarn is woven into an interesting weave with a contrasting warp and weft for additional effect. Although the photographs on the following pages show a commercial loom being used, you can produce equally good results on any type of loom you have access to, from a simple hand loom (ideal for beginners) to an industrial model. The step-by-step guide shows, in brief form, how paper yarn is threaded onto a loom in preparation for weaving. If you wish to use the weave for a lampshade, treat it with a flame retardant first.

Left: Paper yarn or tape can be woven on a loom in much the same way as conventional yarns. This selection of different weaves by Michelle Wild shows an exciting range of effects which can be achieved with flair and experimentation.

Below: A sample of woven paper cut from the loom. The correct side shows the rows in the weave, created by alternating between two different coloured yarns in the weft.

1

2

EQUIPMENT

Warping frame

Loom (a simple hand loom
   is perfectly adequate if
   you do not have access
   to a larger one, as
   shown in the
   photographs here)

Paper yarn

Stick or shuttle

Scissors

1 MAKING THE WARP

The warp (the yarn which
runs along the length of a
cloth) is made by
wrapping the yarn around
a warping frame, forming
a cross at the beginning
and the end of the warp.

2 RADDLING

The warp is then attached
to the back roller. A raddle
is used to space the warp
out across the back of the
loom. This helps to ensure
an even weave.

Remember that your
loom may slightly differ to
the one shown in this
series of photographs so,
if necessary, follow the
manufacturer's
instructions supplied with
the loom instead.

3

3 WINDING ON THE WARP

The next stage is to wind
the warp onto the back
roller of the loom with a
piece of paper carefully
inserted in between so
that the fibres do not sink
into each other.

4 THREADING WARP

The end of the warp is cut and the warp ends individually threaded through the heddles (vertical spindles) on the shafts (the bars which lift the warp yarns).The order in which the threading occurs is instrumental in determining the construction of the weave. The warp is then threaded through the gaps or dents in the reed (an enclosed comb-like device at the front of the loom), thus separating out the threads and helping to denote the thickness of the cloth.

4

5

5 TYING ON

The warp is then tied onto a stick attached to the front roller of the loom, working from the middle outwards, and ensuring an even tension all the way across the loom.

6 WEAVING

The weft (the yarn which runs across the cloth) is wound onto a stick or shuttle (the implement used to thread the weft across the warp). A small amount of waste cloth is then woven in a plain weave in order to compact the warp.

To weave, a selection of ends are lifted by the shafts and the shuttle carrying the weft is passed through the gap (or shed). The shafts are lowered and the beater which houses the reed is pulled forwards to beat up the weft yarn.

The construction of a weave is dependent on the order in which the warp ends are threaded onto the shafts on the loom (called the draft) and the order in which the shafts are lifted (called the peg plan).

Once the desired amount of cloth has been woven, it is then cut off the loom and the loose ends tied into knots. In this demonstration it was more practical for the right side of the design to be woven face-down.

6

CRUMPLING

The practice of manipulating materials to achieve interesting relief finishes is utilised by many contemporary textile designers. They often choose silk as the raw material and employ elaborate processes involving wax, latex and steam to ensure the textures are secured in the fabric.

The same effects can be achieved using paper which, due to its properties, lends itself to this type of treatment, enabling textures to be retained with sharper clarity. It can be folded, crumpled, crinkled and creased and when unravelled, the folds and creases will remain permanently fixed without the need of additional treatment.

An interesting exercise is to practise a number of very simple treatments on a choice of papers and observe the results. Papers such as coloured tissue and writing paper of various weights and fibres will respond differently to the same treatments. When tissue is scrunched into a ball and then unfolded it becomes softer and more pliable. However, when the same treatment is applied to writing paper, sharp angular ridges appear. When rolled into a tube and twisted as if being wrung out, paper will be left with a series of random ribs and crinkles. The repeated action of folding creates a permanent geometrical grid held in the fibres of the sheet. These very simple treatments alter both the surface appearance and the properties of the paper as the fibres are bent and twisted, giving the material a completely new dimension.

Some techniques work more successfully if the paper is soaked. As seen in the demonstration of tie-dye on pages 102-105, the paper is tied, then soaked with ink. Once it has dried, the intricate texture created by this particular tying method is retained in the paper. In ancient Japan, paper was wrinkled by hand and various additives such as oils and root extracts applied to give it surprising strength with a finish resembling leather.

Following in the Japanese tradition, an ingenious but surprisingly simple technique can be applied to paper, creating a material which emulates both the look and feel of a ruched silk fabric. As this process involves saturating the sheet with ink, the appropriate choice of stock is essential, namely a paper which will not tear easily when wet. Handmade lokta paper from Nepal is ideal for this technique as its exceptionally long fibres give the sheet additional strength, especially when wet. In the demonstration shown here, natural lokta paper with an added recycled content of cotton rags is used to stunning effect.

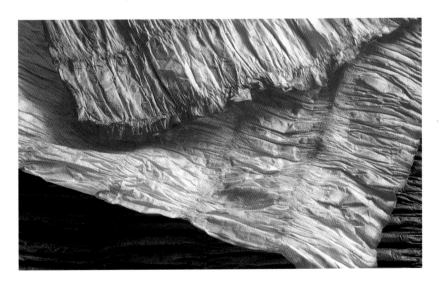

Left: This selection of crumpled papers by Mara Amats and Beata Thackeray shows a finish which can be created with the use of a simple yet effective technique. The paper is first soaked in a subtle range of coloured inks and then manipulated to achieve this surface texture, reminiscent of crushed silk.

Left: Natural lokta paper from Nepal is used for this process as it has just the right properties to create the desired result. This paper is fine enough to be repeatedly wrapped and sufficiently strong to be soaked and crumpled without tearing.

EQUIPMENT

Large sheets of
   hand-made paper
   approximately
   50 x 76 cm (20 x 30 in)
A selection of coloured
   inks
Empty jam jars
Paint brushes
Plastic ruler, 50 cm (20 in)
   long
Protective gloves
   (optional)

Old newspapers, to
   protect the worksurface
   from paint stains

1

2

1 PREPARING TO WRAP

Fold the sheet of paper in
half along its length. The
shortest edge of the sheet
must be no longer than the
ruler. Mix some inks to a
chosen colour and dilute
with a generous amount of
water, depending how
intense you want the
colour to be. Undiluted ink
may cause the paper to
stick when dry. As the
paper is very absorbent, it
is important to have a
generous amount of ink.
An empty jam jar three-
quarters full is sufficient to
soak a few sheets.

   Paint the ink on a small
section of the sheet at one
end of the width. Place the
ruler across the width of
the sheet about 2 mm
(⅛ in) from the edge.

2 DYEING AND
WRAPPING

Roll the ruler over, taking
the paper with it, and fold
it down. Paint the reverse
side of the paper now
laying over the ruler,
ensuring the paper is fully
saturated with the ink.

   Take care not to roll the
paper too tightly around
the ruler, allowing
approximately 2 mm (⅛ in)
of slack either side of the
ruler each time it is turned
and wrapped.

3 CRUMPLING

While the paper is saturated, take hold of the ruler in a vertical position, and carefully press the wrapped paper down its length so that it collapses and wrinkles.

First apply pressure in the centre and then from the top to ease the roll down in order to squash it into about a third of its original height. If the paper is wrapped too tightly and will not move with ease, unroll the sheet and wrap it more loosely.

When using permanent inks it is important to protect your clothes and work space. As the paper is squashed, the ink will invariably ooze out of the folds, so it is advisable to work on a surface of old newspapers. To avoid staining your hands, you may wish to wear protective gloves.

3

4

4 DRYING AND UNRAVELLING

Lay the ruler on a sheet of newspaper to protect surfaces from the wet ink and leave to dry. This may take a day or two depending on the climate. If you wish to accelerate the process, leave it in a warm dry place such as an airing cupboard or near a heater.

When the paper is completely dry, peel it open carefully and unravel the sheet to reveal the crumpled texture.

EMBOSSING

The very nature of paper allows for shapes and textures to be embossed into it as the fibres remain flexible even when dry. In fact, some machine-made papers are sold on the merit of their surface textures, created when a continual sheet is fed through a large embossing roller.

An intricate design can also be impressed into a sheet of paper using a hand-held embossing tool, available from specialist makers (see stockists on pages 154-155). When pressed onto the paper, the fibres are bent into shape following the male and female plates of the tool. With the use of a press

and some imagination, more abstract embossings can be made with simple objects. A thick card such as polyboard or foamboard can also be cut into interesting shapes to create more subtle embossing. In the demonstration on page 85 a length of rope has been used for a simple spiral pattern.

The paper used is made from a river reed called phragmytes (see pages 50-53 for detailed making instructions). Choose a heavy paper that is uncoated and preferably hand-made so that the fibres are less compressed. The more tightly condensed the fibres, the less effective the result. For instance, a blotting paper will be more easily embossed than a highly coated art paper.

Below: These attractive embossings created by Michelle Wild are made using decorative shapes cut from card and placed on sheets of thick hand-made paper. The sheets are then passed through a small printing press.

1

2

EQUIPMENT

Sheet of thick hand-made
    paper (see introduction
    on facing page for
    details of suitable
    papers)

Large paste brush

Water pot

Length of heavyweight
    rope

Book or flower press

1 PREPARING THE
PAPER

Dampen the sheet with
water using the paste
brush to give the paper
added flexibility. However,
take care not to over-
saturate the fibres and
thus weaken the paper. If
the paper is lightly sized,
there is less chance that it
will tear when pressed
over an object.

2 EMBOSSING USING A
PRESS

It is important to select a
suitable object from which
to emboss. It must be
flexible so that it does not
break under pressure
when placed in the press.
One very effective,
everyday item to start
experimenting with is rope
of different weights and
thicknesses.

Coil a length of rope
into a spiral and lay it on a
dampened sheet of paper.
To make a simultaneous
impression on two sheets,
lay another dampened
sheet on top.

Place the sandwich of
the two sheets and the
rope in the press. The
actual pressing time will
depend on the paper and
the type of pressing tool. If

using a book press, leave
the sheets in the press
overnight and then lay the
papers out to dry.

RECYCLED DESIGN

RIGHT

Lois Walpole is a British artist who combines various found materials and recycles them to stunning effect to make her wide range of functional pieces. This bowl is an excellent example of her work. The colourful bright weave is achieved by the choice of materials, in this case, glossy leaflets, telephone wire and electric cable.

BELOW RIGHT

The Crowing Cockerel is by artist Heidrun Guest of Paper Works, in Totnes, Devon. Through this piece the artist aims to advertise the recycling of paper. Made of papier mâché, she uses the technique of layering paper based on a balloon and cone shape. The materials used include scraps of newspaper, wallpaper paste and wire.

LEFT

Clare Goddard, a British designer, utilises reclaimed materials to create her unusual fabrics. This piece, entitled *Tea Bag Handbag*, as the name suggests features handbags made from tea bag fabric. This unique material is produced using tea bag paper which is coloured, waterproofed and then laminated onto a backing cloth. It is then constructed into a handbag form.

RIGHT

These unique shirts from a series named *Body Emballage* by artist Annette Meyer are made out of recycled paper wrappings from Denmark, Japan and USA. By using paper packaging to make clothes, the material is endowed with a new function and the graphic elements take on another meaning, from informative to a decorative pattern. Crumpling and ironing the paper creates a material with a soft textured surface well suited to making short-life clothes.

BELOW

This sculptural piece created by Dutch artist Marian Smit is made of recycled magazines. The paper is rolled into tubes which are glued, painted and varnished. The elements are connected by copper wire to form this exciting three-dimensional structure.

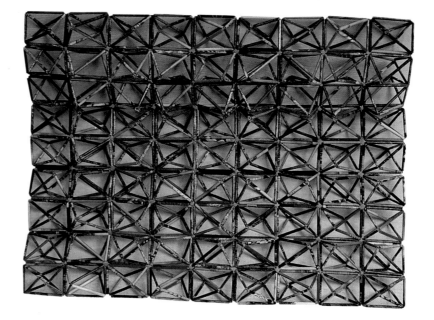

Right: This piece by Mara Amats shows how a number of different pulp mixtures can be combined on one surface and couched to form a single sheet. This technique demands patience and skill in the handling of wet pulp fibres.

EMBEDDING WITH PULP

Paper pulp in its wet form can be used in a variety of ways to create unique papers with interesting textures. A number of separate layers of fibres can be couched on top of one another to achieve a thicker sheet. If sheets made of two separate pulp mixes of different colours are couched on top of one another, the resulting paper will be one colour on one side and a different colour on the other. The top layer of fibres may be watermarked leaving a coloured shadow where the base paper is revealed.

Pulp can be applied in an arrangement of shapes, building up an interesting composition of colour and texture. There are artists who have perfected the technique of painting with coloured pulp by spraying it onto a canvas with the use a pulp sprayer and compressor.

The following demonstration shows a technique involving the use of different types of pulp combined in one layer of fibres to make a single sheet of paper. When preparing the different pulp mixtures, it is important that the main source of fibre is the same otherwise it may be difficult to achieve good bonding. The pulp is varied by use of colour and added ingredients. Here the two pulp mixtures, both derived from the phragmytes plant, vary in tone and brightness as one is bleached and the other unbleached. Refer to the section on advanced papermaking on pages 50-53 to see how the pulp is prepared using phragmytes fibre. Also see pages 48-49 in the section on intermediate papermaking, where various techniques involving adding colour and texture to paper pulp are explored.

1 ISOLATING AREAS AND POURING THE PULP

Start by preparing the different pulp mixtures and add the bleached pulp to a vat filled with warm water. Then dilute the unbleached pulp in the jug with a small amount of water to a porridge-like consistency.

Plan the pattern you wish to make and find objects which will help to achieve it. It is advisable to begin with simple geometric shapes. Here, plastic trays are used to mask off two areas on the face of the mould and are held down with heavy paperweights to keep them in place.

Hold the mould over the vat with one hand and, with the other hand, use a jug or other empty container to scoop up some of the water and pulp mixture from the vat. Carefully pour it over the areas around the objects on the mould until the exposed mesh is completely covered with a thick layer of pulp.

1

2

EQUIPMENT

Vat filled with bleached pulp and water mixture
Mould and deckle
Jug with unbleached pulp and water
Pouring jug
Plastic trays
Paper weights
Short ruler
Felts
Press

2 DRAINING THE MOULD

Place the mould on the side of the vat to allow as much water as possible to drain off, leaving a thick blanket of fibres. Very carefully remove the objects, ensuring that the edges of the pulp stay firm and do not collapse into the vacant spaces left on the mesh.

3 ADDING THE SECOND PULP MIXTURE

The second pulp mixture should be a thick consistency, diluted with a small amount of water. Pour the pulp into the exposed areas of the mesh, gently butting up the second set of fibres against the first layer. If necessary, use your fingers to coax the pulp into place. Do not worry if the two types of pulp blend into each other, as at this stage you are working on the reverse side of the sheet.

3

COUCHING THE SHEET
See Papermaking, pages 46-47

4 CREATING STRIPES

To be even more adventurous, mark off sections of one of the vacant areas using a ruler to create stripes, filling them alternately with different pulp as you cover the space. Once all the exposed areas are covered, carefully remove the deckle and prepare to couch your sheet.

Finish the procedure by pressing the sheet and drying it in the usual way. For full instructions on couching refer to the intermediate papermaking on pages 46 and 47.

4

PAPER PULP ARTWORKS

This wall sculpture entitled *True Colours* is by American artist Lin Fife. It has been made using dyed, formed hand-made paper. The pulp has been produced from dyed cotton fibre and the surface of the piece treated by being hand-pressed to achieve a rough texture.

The American artist Mildred Fischer uses pulp derived from linen and kozo fibres to produce her stunning designs. The piece entitled *Quadratum*, is made up of four sheets of hand-made paper.

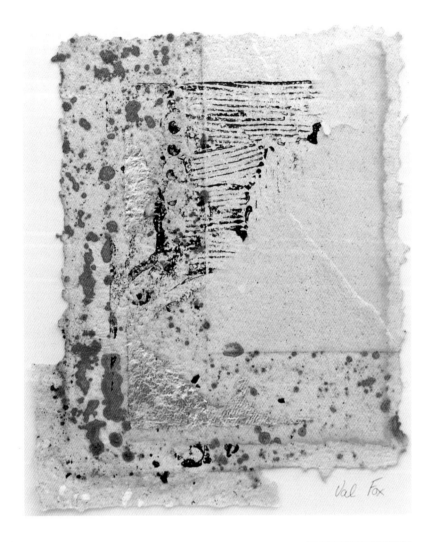

ABOVE LEFT AND RIGHT

British artist Val Fox has combined recycled paper pulp with dried spices to create the subtle palette for this series, entitled *Fragments*. Paprika, coriander and cumin provide earthy organic shades while turmeric adds a rich yellow hue. To create the collages, the papers are selected, shapes and textures chosen and juxtaposed. The papers are printed upon, manipulated and placed together with constructed objects which leave an imprint, or rusty metals which leave a residue upon them.

BELOW LEFT

The American artist John Babcock has developed what he calls free-cast paper. He uses pulp of his own manufacture to create art works of cast, inlaid and collaged papers. Different fibres are combined when building the pieces as they reflect and absorb light in a variety of ways. The artist uses a mix of fibres, including cotton, abaca, banana stalk and kozo, to make up a number of pulp mixes which are then pigmented. Sometimes pulps in as many as thirty different hues are used.

APPLYING SURFACE DECORATION

Paper provides a perfect canvas for the application of decorative techniques. Some of these have a long tradition dating back through the centuries to ancient Japan and Persia. In this section we cover some of these processes, including the technique of dyeing, firstly with the art of folding and dyeing paper and then progressing to the more familiar tie-dye process.

Pigments may be applied to and manipulated on a paper's surface in a variety of ways to create differing patterns, as illustrated by the techniques of paste painting and marbling.

There are now numerous mechanised printing processes, but the early methods of lino printing, etching and wood block are traditional hand processes steeped in history. These are still practised by many contemporary artists and printers. One of these techniques, wood block printing using a traditional Japanese method, is included here.

Other techniques featured here include the use of stencils to create layers of pattern with coloured paper pulp. Various metallic finishes are achieved with the application of different media, from inks and paints to gold and silver leaf. The first technique to be demonstrated is collage, where found papers are combined and arranged in attractive layouts.

COLLAGE

The art of collage involves bringing together random materials which are subsequently arranged and layered to create new and unique images, patterns and textures. Collage is a highly individual medium. As with most artistic expression, a number of different artists given the same subject matter and media, will produce as many varied results unique and original to them.

This technique has a number of practical applications. It can be used to decorate interiors or articles of furniture which can then be sealed with varnish. Simple household items such as picture frames and vases can be enriched with added colour and texture. A popular use for collage is in the production of greetings cards and stationery items.

In the following demonstration a wide variety of found papers are used and combined to stunning effect to produce a range of unique cards. The materials include packaging for Chinese tea and soaps, old prints, dolls' house papers, out-of-date maps, plus foils such as Easter egg and sweet wrappers. Coloured tissue is used to enhance laminated effects and hand-made papers painted with acrylic paints.

Left: This collection of collage designs by Jane Millar shows the many different found papers which can be combined and decorated to create fresh compositions both stunning and intricate in their detail.

EQUIPMENT

An array of found papers

Acrylic paints

Paint brushes

Mounting card

Strong paper glue
   (not water-based)

Scissors or craft knife

1 PREPARING THE BACKGROUNDS

Select the choice of papers to be worked on, considering their colours and contrasting surface textures and finishes. These can then be further embellished with areas of painted colour and pieces of coloured foil glued on as shown in the photograph below.

1

2 CREATING THE LAYERS

Begin to add elements to the surfaces. This can be done in an infinite number of ways - the only restraint is your imagination, so experiment until you find combinations of shapes, textures and colours that appeal to you.

Here paper shapes have been cut from pieces of mounting card and applied to the chosen surface. A layer of tissue paper or foil has then been placed on top. Smooth the paper over the shapes beneath to reveal the different contours.

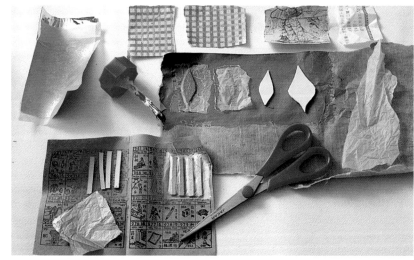

2

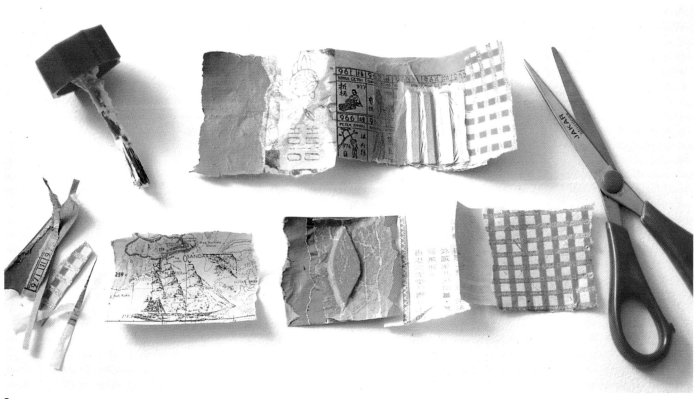

3

3 COMPOSING THE LAYOUT

Create many surfaces, then assemble them by colour, texture and pattern. The chosen elements are torn down into manageable sized pieces to give them an attractive ragged edge and then arranged in a chosen order.

When the desired layout has been achieved, glue the various elements into position and neatly trim the edges of the finished piece.

CARDS AND COLLAGE

BELOW

The French designer Caroline Burzynski-Delloye produces these cards made from plain coloured sheets of paper. The designs are achieved simply by cutting a well-planned arrangement of incisions along a central fold in the paper. When opened up, a three-dimensional image is revealed, enhanced by the play of light and shadow on the cuts and folds.

RIGHT

Mark Hill, a British artist, has designed these very elegant greetings cards using a simple yet effective collage technique. Gold and silver leaf are combined with an assortment of carefully pressed dried flower petals to create a multi-layered image.

LE LION

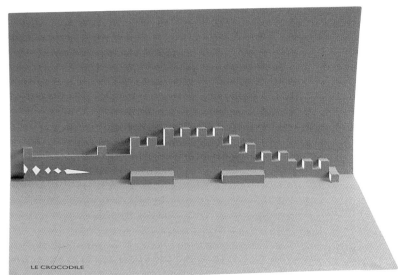

LE CROCODILE

ABOVE
This greeting card, entitled *Oranges and Lemons* by British artist Sarah Hamilton, is made using Somerset paper. The image is created by silkscreening water-based screen inks with the use of paper stencils.

RIGHT
These cards, designed by Beata Thackeray, demonstrate a marriage of Eastern traditions with Western aesthetics. They were produced at the Udyog paper project in Bangladesh using paper made by the village women's cooperative. The paper was made from jute waste and the dyes derived from natural ingredients. Traditional hand-carved wood blocks used for printing cloth were adapted to produce these subtle and decorative details.

EQUIPMENT

Absorbent paper (see
   introduction on the right
   for more details)

Bulldog clips

Coloured inks

Ink pots

FOLD AND DYE

This technique of *Itajime-zome*, as it is known in Japan, is a simple introduction to creating patterns with the use of dyes. It is still practised today for dyeing both cloth and paper. The Japanese dampen the material, fold it in different ways and press it between two carved wooden blocks. It is then dipped in a vat of dye. When applied to paper the patterns can appear crisp and well defined, characteristic in their linear quality.

In the photographs shown here, a simpler method is shown with the folded paper held together using bulldog clips and the corners and sides of the concertina dipped into dishes of different coloured dyes. It is best to use an absorbent paper which has not been coated. Here a hand-made paper using jute fibre from Bangladesh has been chosen for its creamy tone and absorbent quality.

Use a maximum of three colours to create the patterns. It is best to use pale tones with one darker hue to achieve a subtle effect. Here a pale turquoise blue and muted shade of brown are highlighted with a hint of darker brown. If applied to coloured papers, the same range of inks will create yet more varied results.

1 FOLDING

Begin by experimenting with small pieces of A5 size paper (210 x 148 mm/ 8¼ x 5¾ in). Fold the paper twice along its length and then unfold to make a concertina using the creased lines as a guide.

For a simple effect, this long strip can be folded repeatedly along the width to make a square concertina. As shown here, a more complex concertina resulting in a small folded triangle can also be made.

This is done by laying the strip lengthways and bringing the bottom left corner up to meet the top of the strip. The edge of the width should now correspond to the top edge of the length, making a right-angled triangle. Fold across the diagonal and turn the strip over. Bend the far corner of the triangle over the bottom edge of the strip and make a vertical fold. Repeat until you reach the end of the strip. Trim away any excess paper to leave a neatly folded triangle.

1

2

2 DIPPING AND DYEING

Mix the inks into three colours which complement each other. These can be diluted for paler tones. Attach a bulldog clip to the triangle concertina (to hold the folds together and to act as a handle) and dip each corner into a different ink. Unfold to see the result.

To create lines, dip the paper triangle in the ink along one or more of the edges of the folds. Crosses or circles can be made by dipping the corners. More intricate and layered patterns can be made if the process of folding and dipping is repeated. Leaving the paper to dry completely between dipping will give a crisp result.

For a softer effect, fold the paper when partly dry so that the inks will blend into each other. A variety of different patterns can be achieved depending on the amount of ink allowed to seep into the paper, the number of times the paper is dipped, and the order in which the colours are applied to the paper.

TIE-DYE

Tie-dye or, as it is known in Japan, *Shibori-zome* is the art of tying pieces of material, most commonly silk, cotton or paper, with thread and dipping them in dye. The points where the threads are tied are untouched by the dye, creating patterns characteristic of this technique.

In Japan, a strong hand-made paper called *momogami* was traditionally treated with a starch and wrinkled specifically for the purpose. These papers had a number of uses, including purses and book covers. Very fine patterns could be achieved by using bamboo sticks which would be pressed into the paper at closely spaced points. As the paper was wrapped over the ends and tied, the sticks were removed. Once the papers were dyed and the threads untied, the texture created in the paper was retained, giving the impression of ruched silk.

The papers would be used as hair decorations by the poorer classes who could not afford the more lavish silk versions. Despite the hours of intricate work required to produce them, very few examples of these papers remain as they were often discarded after use. The photograph of The Parkes' Collection of Japanese papers on page 13 shows some examples which have survived the years.

EQUIPMENT

Hand-made paper,
    approximately
    20 x 25 cm (8 x 10 in)
Pencil
Ruler
Rice grains
Thread
Coloured ink or fabric dye
Paint brush
Stanley knife
Iron (optional)

Left: Tie-dye is a technique most commonly applied to cloth. However, a thin but strong hand-made paper such as this lokta paper from Nepal can be tied and dyed to create fine rings of colour. By its very nature, paper retains creases and so the surface texture created by the action of tying can be preserved once the paper is dry, as shown in these papers by Beata Thackeray.

1

2

2 TYING THE FIRST KNOT

Wind a large amount of thread onto a small bobbin or folded piece of paper. Lay the sheet reverse side up, take a grain of rice and place it on the paper pointing into the first dot marked on the sheet, either top right or top left.

Carefully gather the paper and pinch it around the rice grain. Wrap the thread around the base of the rice grain to enclose it securely in the paper, tie a knot and wind the thread around ten times. Do not cut the thread.

1 DRAWING THE POINTS

Draw a grid of horizontal and vertical lines no less than 4 cm (1¾ in) apart on the reverse side of the sheet of paper. On the correct side of the sheet, draw a dot at each point where the lines cross.

3

3 TYING THE SECOND KNOT

Repeat the process at the next dot on the sheet, taking care to allow some slack in the thread, equal to the distance between the two points.

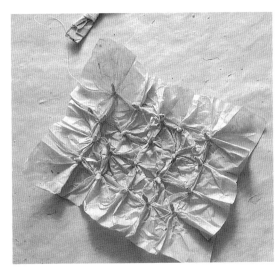

4

4 TYING ACROSS THE GRID

Proceed across the grid of dots, working along the first row then down to the next, with one continual thread. You will notice that the paper begins to crease and fold into an attractive ruched pattern.

5 DYEING THE SHEET

Once the whole sheet has been tied, it is ready to be dyed. Depending on the absorbency of the paper, it can either be dipped into a small tray of dye or the colour painted on with a brush. A number of tones of the same colour can be applied to different parts of the sheet to give the pattern a feeling of depth.

As shown in the photograph, the tied points have been left without any dye to accentuate the relief texture of the paper.

Choose a water-based pigment such as a coloured ink or fabric dye which will be easily absorbed into the fibres of the paper. Ink should be diluted with water to prevent the paper from sticking together and tearing when dry.

5

6

6 UNTYING THE SHEET

Leave the sheet to dry (this may take a day or two). If you wish to accelerate the process, leave the paper near a heat source such as boiler or in an airing cupboard, laying it on a sheet of newspaper to avoid unwanted stains.

When the sheet is absolutely dry, cut the threads with the knife and pull away. The paper can be opened slightly, retaining the ruched texture. Alternatively, you may choose to flatten the sheet by pressing it with a warm iron to reveal the fine rings of colour.

PASTE PAINTING

Paste painting is the decorative technique of applying thick paint to the surface of paper and manipulating it to create patterns. It was traditionally practiced by bookbinders who created their own designs for endpapers in hand-bound books.

The most important aspect of this craft is the choice of colours. Simple designs can be created using a single colour or combining two colours which, when blended together, will produce a third. For the more adventurous, designs may be built up using three colours. Muted tones are the most elegant, evoking a feeling of antiquity.

In these photos, oxide colours of iron and cobalt are combined with stunning effect, as well as deep tones of purple, brown and royal blue. The paints can either be applied to a white sheet or to a striped and coloured base. The patterns created in the wet paint are suggested by the implements used, for example graining tools make sharp defined patterns which can be complemented with a softer swirling effect created by smudging the paint using a finger.

The best choice of paper to use for paste painting is a thin weight of cartridge which is strong enough to hold a lot of moisture but without being too absorbent.

EQUIPMENT

Thin cartridge paper

Old newspaper

Acrylic poster paints

Wallpaper paste
   (fungicide-free) or flour
   and water mixture

Selection of paint brushes,
   minimum 2.5 cm (1 in)
   in width

Combing and graining
   tools

PREPARING THE PAINT

It is best to use acrylic or poster paint in rich, saturated colours. The secret of this technique is to work quickly before the paint is able to dry.

It is advisable to mix the paint with a simple solution of flour and water or wallpaper paste, preferably without additives such as fungicide. This helps to prolong the drying time and also gives the paint a thicker consistency, thus making it easier to manipulate. Use approximately one quarter paste to three-quarters paint. When mixed, the mixture should be of a painting consistency. Try it out first on scrap paper.

PASTE PATTERNS ON A PLAIN BACKGROUND

1 APPLYING THE STRIPES

Choose a paper which is either white or a plain colour. Place your sheet on a worksurface covered with old newspapers. Paint evenly spaced, vertical stripes about 4 cm (1½ in) wide.

With a clean brush, apply the second colour to create a pattern of alternate coloured stripes. Blend the paints by slightly overlapping them.

2 SMUDGING

Now is the time to work quickly so that the paint does not dry. From the base of the page run the tip of your index finger along one of the stripes in a spiral motion, rubbing into the paint as you go. This will create a soft, coiled, three-dimensional pattern effect as the paint is smudged.

1

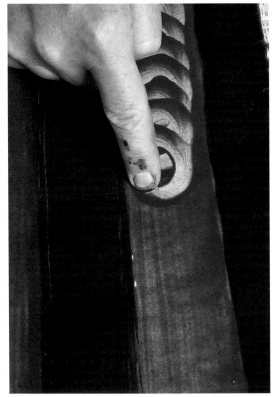

2

3 SCRAPING

To create a contrasting effect, choose a tool with sharp teeth, such as a broken section of a comb or a rubber wood-graining tool. Scrape into the paint by running the teeth along the wet surface in straight or curved lines, revealing the base colour of the paper. Experiment on a number of sheets with various scraping patterns, adding interest by overlapping the different markings.

3

PASTE PATTERNS ON A PATTERNED BACKGROUND

1 PREPARING THE PAINTED SURFACE

Choose two colours and apply them to your paper in wide horizontal stripes. Do not mix these colours with a paste solution as these will be worked on when dry. Allow the sheet to dry.

A third colour mixed with the paste is applied over the dry horizontal stripes, covering the whole sheet with a thick layer of paint.

2 CREATING THE PATTERN

With a straight-edged implement such as a piece of card or rubber, scrape away sections of the top layer of paint to leave vertical stripes of wet colour. Work into the remaining stripes with various combing and graining tools, overlapping the different patterns. The degree of pressure exerted with the tools will affect the way the paint reacts, giving an even greater scope of variety as the wet surface is manipulated.

1

2

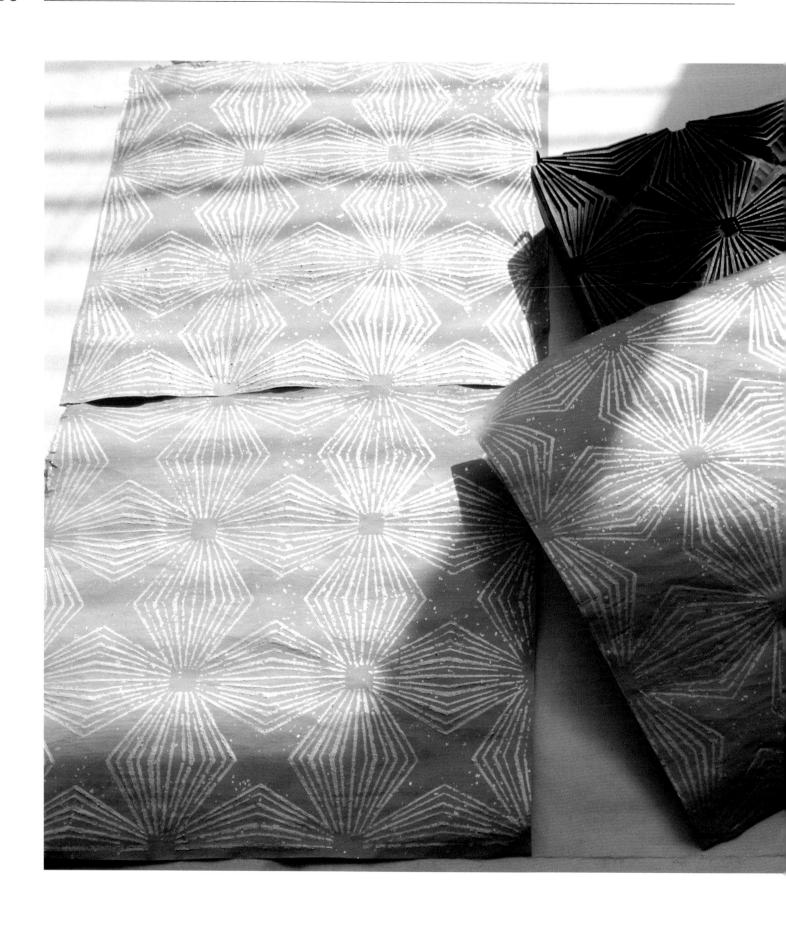

WOOD BLOCK PRINTING

Paper is used to great effect in the traditional Japanese home where living spaces are separated by moveable sliding panels. These panels, known as *shoji*, are constructed from sheets of hand-made paper which are stretched and glued onto wooden frames. Light can shine through the translucent paper, creating a warm glow throughout the interior of the home.

Many different types of *shoji* have been developed, including *fusuma-shoji* which is covered in thick paper, while *karakami-shoji* is coated with paper printed in patterns of colour and mica. This feature, dating back to ancient Japan, was to influence western architecture in a profound way. *Fusuma* are still used today in many Japanese homes. The *fusuma* paper is usually made from *kozo*, a plant native to Japan and one of the three main plant ingredients used in traditional Japanese hand papermaking.

The step-by-step demonstration shown on the following pages faithfully recreates the traditional method of block printing the *karakami* paper, using authentic Japanese papers, ingredients and utensils to create a subtle and delicate surface decoration.

EQUIPMENT

Gofun paint

Raw umber pigment

Sheet of glass

Glass muller

Sheet of Japanese kozo
    paper, cut to fit the
    dimensions of the wood
    block

Wide brush

Gold leaf

Bamboo tube and brush

Mica powder

Seaweed

Palette knife for mixing
    paint

Wooden hoop covered
    with a fine piece of silk

Wood block

1

2

3

1 PREPARING THE SHEET

Gofun paint is made from oyster shells which have been pounded to a powder with a mortar and pestle and then mixed with rice starch paint which has been cooked and then strained through a sieve.

Pigments are then added to the paint. These are traditionally umber, indigo, lamp black (made of soot) and yellow ochre. The gofun paint used here has been mixed with raw umber. It is spread onto a glass sheet using a glass muller and, with a wide brush, painted in a thick layer onto a sheet of Japanese kozo. The paint is mainly for decorative effect, rendering the sheet of paper opaque.

2 APPLYING THE GOLD LEAF

While the sheet is still wet, the decorative gold leaf is added. This is traditionally applied through a wide bamboo tube, with the bottom opening covered with a fine mesh. A sheet of gold leaf is placed inside the tube and gently pushed through the mesh by the brush, so that it sprinkles onto the paper.

The paper is then left to dry thoroughly overnight.

3 MIXING THE PRINTING INK

Mix the mica powder and seaweed on a sheet of glass with the palette knife to form the printing ink. This should have a thick, smooth consistency. The seaweed is in a gel form, extracted from the dried seaweed by gentle heating and straining.

4

4 INKING THE WOOD BLOCK

The ink is traditionally applied to the wood block through a wooden hoop, similar to a circular sewing frame, wrapped in silk. The mica ink is applied to the surface of the silk and tapped gently over the wood block's surface, allowing a fine coating of mica to pass through the silk onto the raised areas of the block.

5

5 PRINTING THE PAPER

In this demonstration, the prepared paper is carefully laid onto the wood block. In the more conventional way, the block is laid into position on the printing surface.

The paper is pressed gently onto the block with the palms and fingers, transferring the paint from the block to the paper. This method ensures a crisp finish to the printed areas, avoiding blots along the edges of the wood block lines, which is characteristic of the more common method.

The sheet is carefully peeled away from the block by picking up one corner and drawing it back and away from the block. In a warm room, the paper will dry within three hours.

When dry, the creamy paper displays the silver texture of the mica ink.

MARBLING

The technique of marbling developed in Japan was called *sumi-nagashi*, meaning 'ink flow'. The finest examples date back to 1100. Coloured inks called *sumi* were floated on water in rings, fanned into ripples resembling a flowing stream, and then transferred to a sheet of hand-made paper. The papers were traditionally used for poetry.

In the fifteenth century a similar technique was developed in Persia, using size to float and manipulate oil-based paints into intricate patterns. The craft spread to Italy, France and Holland, finally reaching Britain in 1625. The marbled sheets were used as endpapers and covers for bookbinding. For many centuries the technique was kept a secret and in order to preserve the mystery, no single person in a bindery would know or execute the entire process. It was not until the early twentieth century that marblers began to share their knowledge.

EQUIPMENT

Shallow tank (or clean cat litter tray)

Courlose powder

Oil paint in tubes (students' oils are the most suitable)

Paint pots

White spirit

Oxgall (or washing up liquid)

Paint brushes

Stylus or small knitting needle

Paper (kraft and coloured paper)

Paper press or heavy weights

Strips of newspaper

Carragheen moss

Cooking pot

Sieve

Borax (or water softener)

Bucket

Combs

MARBLING WITH GLUE SIZE

1 PREPARING THE SIZE

Fill a shallow tank with cool water. Add 15-20 ml (3-4 teaspoons) of courlose powder to the water and mix it in thoroughly. It is possible to use standard wallpaper paste, but many brands now include a fungicide which will not work with the paints.

The size mixture should resemble the consistency of a runny honey. This can be varied slightly, depending on the intended pattern. To create loose swirls, the size needs to be easily manipulated and thinner than for a combed pattern, for which a greater degree of control is required.

2

3

4

2 MIXING THE PAINTS

Decide the order for adding colours to the size. This is crucial, affecting the pattern as the paints build up in layers and the mixing sequence.

Squeeze some paint from each tube into separate containers and thin down gradually with small amounts of white spirit until the paints are runny. For the best results, do not use turpentine or turpentine substitute in place of white spirit.

Taking the first colour in the sequence, add a few small drops of oxgall. A slightly larger quantity of oxgall is added to the next colour, even more to the third, and so on.

Oxgall affects the behaviour of the paints once applied to the size. Washing-up liquid also performs the same function of reducing the water's surface tension and allowing the paint drops to spread.

It is possible to control the spreading of the paints by mixing them correctly. If the paint is too thick it will sink, too thin and it will spread more than necessary.

3 APPLYING THE PAINT

Dip the brush into the first colour and squeeze against the pot's edge to remove excess paint. The paint is spattered onto the surface of the size. Build up colours by spattering them one by one, covering the area evenly with fine droplets. Here, green paint is applied first followed by cream, then blue-grey and finally deep mossy green. The droplets of paint begin to disperse as they land on the surface of the size. If a blob appears that does not immediately begin to disperse, gently blow on it.

4 CREATING A PATTERN

The paint spattered in this way creates an interesting random pattern and can be immediately transferred onto a sheet of paper (see steps 5 and 6). Alternatively, the surface of the size can be manipulated further to form a decorative pattern.

Choose a sharp implement such as a small knitting needle to act as a stylus, and sink the point below the surface of the size. Run the point through the paint, dragging it into a series of attractive loose swirls and coils.

5

6

5 LAYING DOWN THE SHEET

To transfer the pattern onto paper, hold the sheet at diagonal corners and carefully lay down the end closest to you on top of the size. Smooth the paper gently over the size without disturbing the surface. Avoid trapping air under the sheet as this will leave a gap in the pattern.

6 TAKING OFF THE SHEET

Immediately the sheet is laid down it can be removed safe in the knowledge that the pattern has transferred with all its fine detail.

Pick the two nearest adjacent corners and drag the paper towards you, scraping it over the edge of the tank to deposit the excess size from the sheet back into the solution. Miraculously, the pattern will remain intact on the surface of the paper.

7

7 CLEANING THE SIZE

It is vital that after marbling a sheet, the surface of the size is cleaned of residue paint or fluff that may ruin the next pattern. Once the sheet is removed from the tank, run a strip of newspaper over the entire surface of the size to clean away every last drop of paint before starting the next pattern. This can also be started while the sheet is in the tank. Lay strips of newspaper over the exposed areas of size, picking up the excess paint.

8

8 DRYING THE SHEET

The sheet is then hung to dry, preferably over a waterproof surface as the paper will drip considerably. Some marblers rinse their sheets with clean water, but this is not vital. Depending on the temperature and humidity of the room you work in, the papers may need to be left to dry overnight.

Once dry, the sheets are then pressed flat in a book press or beneath any other suitable pressing tool, such as bricks or heavy weights.

1

Above: A collection of exquisite hand-marbled papers by Solveig Stone of Compton Marbling. The top sheet is the actual sample made during the following demonstration of marbling with carragheen moss. The pattern is created by a sequence of manipulations, starting with feathering, then combing and swirling.

MARBLING WITH CARRAGHEEN MOSS

Carragheen moss, a type of seaweed grown in Ireland, is available in a dried and cut form from marbling or artists' supply shops. This type of size allows the marbled patterns to appear sharp and more defined, ideal for traditional combed patterns.

The formal pattern featured here comprises three separate manipulations, although each of these can be used separately to achieve different patterns. The paints are applied in the same way as for marbling with glue size, by being spattered in a particular sequence. In the demonstration shown here, blue is applied first, followed by maroon, then cream, blue-grey and finally green.

1 PREPARING THE CARRAGHEEN MOSS SIZE

Place 225 g (½ lb) moss and 11 litres (20 pints) water in a large cooking pot and bring it to the boil slowly over a six-hour period. This slow cooking will extract the gelatine.

Soften the water by adding 30 g (6 teaspoons) borax. Drain the gelatin into a bucket through a fine sieve covered with a piece of muslin.

Pour the gelatin into the tank, then gradually dilute it with an equal amount of cool, clean water.

The temperature combined with the consistency of the size can effect the behaviour of the paints. An experienced marbler would spend time arriving at the correct balance, so for the beginner, patience is necessary.

2 MIX AND APPLY PAINTS TO SIZE

Mix the chosen paints and spread them on the size. For detailed instructions, refer to steps 2 and 3 on page 115.

3

4

3 FEATHERING

To produce a feathered effect, a stylus is run back and forth across the width of the tank in a continuous stroke, covering the whole surface from right to left.

4 COMBING

A comb is run across the length of the tank, dragging the paint to create a distinctive effect.

The combing utensil used here comprises a length of wood with protruding nails spaced along it. There are three standard spacings to choose from, the coarsest and most easy to use being 1 cm (½ in) apart, then 5 mm (¼ in), while the most difficult to control is 2 mm (⅛ in).

5 SWIRLING

You may wish to leave the pattern in this regimented combed effect or alternatively, give it an added dimension by running a clean stylus over the ridges created by the comb, picking up the paint in loose swirls.

6 MARBLING THE SHEET

Following steps 5-8 on pages 116-117, transfer the pattern to a clean sheet of paper, drag it off the tank and hang it to dry.

5

MARBLING

Right: Many contemporary marblers continue the long trradition of their craft, recreating the classic marbled patterns used across Europe for many centuries. These fine examples are produced by Colleen Grysparat.

The earliest decorated papers used as endpapers for bookbinding were marbled. The Persians were the first to make use of this paper in books and examples are found in fine manuscripts dating back to the sixteenth century. The art of marbling spread from Persia and Turkey into Europe via Italy and Spain, finally reaching Germany and France by the seventeenth century. Trade between Germany and Britain flourished at this time and it is thought that the marbled papers first brought to England as wrappings for toys were sold to bookbinders who would carefully unwrap them and use them for bindings and for lining boxes. The Dutch were the first to marble the edges of their books.

Right: Shown here is an example from the wide range of marbled papers made by Solveig Stone of Compton Marbling. Solveig uses oil-based paints floated on carragheen size and supplies papers by the sheets, as well as applying them to a range of stationery items.

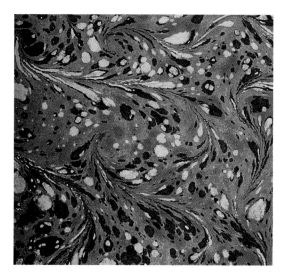

If you are not versed in the history of marbling, you may be forgiven for thinking that these seemingly random patterns are arrived at by happy accident, but some of the patterns which appear as abstract spatterings of colour have a long history.

There are a number of traditional patterns which have been developed and used in Europe since the seventeenth century. Fine combed patterns were perfected in France and superseded by the coarser combed pattern known as Old Dutch. The French curl or Snail pattern was popular across Europe, as was the Moiré effect developed in Spain. Turpentine was added to the colour giving a veined pattern known as Stormont. By the end of the eighteenth century the French Shell pattern was achieved by adding oil to the paint. This caused a drop of colour to form within the shell of another. By the nineteenth century the combed technique was enjoying a revival and these new patterns were known as Nonpareil. The famous and arguably most accomplished marbler of our century was the English bookbinder Douglas Cockerell. Today, many talented marblers across Europe and America continue the long tradition, producing both classic and contemporary designs.

Right: The British artist Victoria Hall produces a wide range of superb marbled papers. Shown here is a small selection of her decorative papers which she makes primarily for use in bookbinding. Victoria uses water-based paints floated on carragheen size to create her modern designs. She also produces fine copies of antiquarian originals which are used in the refurbishment of old bindings.

METALLIC FINISHES

There are many different media which are made up of metal compounds and which can be used to create striking metallic finishes. These range from powders to spray paint, and acrylic inks to metallic leaf, all with their own features and finished effects, and varied applications. As well as paper, a number of materials can be treated with these metallic finishes for decorative effect, including ceramics, wood and metals.

The four examples featured here and on the following pages show the application of various metallic media. The first step demonstrates the use of metallic paints, the second features goldfinger and gold leaf, the third uses metallic powders, and the final step shows decorating with spray paint and glass relief outliner combined with gold metallic tissue.

Glass relief outliner is a metallic paste which is supplied in a tube with a long, thin nozzle. It can be squeezed out in a thin line, rather like decorating a cake with an icing bag. It imitates leaded windows when used on glass or fine strips of silver or gold jewellery, and produces equally stunning results when used on paper.

Goldfinger is a gold paste available in a tube. It is designed to be rubbed with the finger onto objects such as picture frames. As it is spirit-based and contains gold or copper powder, it is advisable to wear rubber gloves to protect the fingers when applying it. An extremely versatile product, goldfinger can also be thinned and used as a paint, applied with a brush.

Right, above and below: These beautiful pieces by Lynne Robinson and Richard Lowther depict the richness and variety of finishes which can be achieved with the use of various metallic media.

1 USING METALLIC PAINTS

EQUIPMENT

Coloured glasene

Graph paper divided into
2.5 cm (1 in) squares

Gold and silver metallic
paints

Paint brushes

Scalpel

Lay a sheet of coloured glasene over the graph paper and paint alternate squares with gold paint. When dry, turn the paper over. In the centre of each of the gold squares, paint silver squares about half their size.

When the paint is dry, rest the glasene on a suitable cutting surface and cut two diagonal slits across each of the silver squares using a scalpel. Turn the paper face up, pull the cut sections out and fold them back, creating a decorative grid.

1

2 USING GOLDFINGER AND GOLD LEAF

EQUIPMENT

Coloured recycled paper

Low-tack masking tape

Coloured acrylic gesso

Combing implement

Goldfinger

Rubber stamp

Ink

Sheet of gold leaf

Small piece of sponge and
card

2

With tape, mask off evenly spaced stripes 4.5 cm (1½ in) apart on the paper. Apply the gesso in a thick layer to the exposed areas and comb a curved pattern through the wet gesso. When the gesso has dried, squeeze some goldfinger from the tube and rub it into the gesso. Remove the tape.

Dip a simple cut rubber stamp in ink and print onto the stripes. Squares of gold leaf are applied by gluing a small square of sponge to a piece of card (to act as a handle), dip it into the size and apply it to the gold leaf (refer to step 7 on page 131 for application instructions).

3

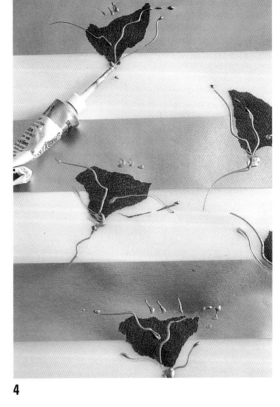

4

3 USING METALLIC POWDERS

EQUIPMENT

Sheet of heavyweight
   paper
Masking tape
Blue and red acrylic paint
Paint brushes
Ready-made paper pulp
Ruler
Trowel
Paper stencil
Metallic super-fine
   powder in bronze,
   green and red
Items to use as stamps
   (screw heads, sealing
   wax sticks, etc)

Begin by deciding the
layout for your final image.
When working with wet
pulp you must act quickly
as the drying time may be
as little as half an hour. To
stop the paper buckling,
stretch and tape it to the
worksurface first. On the
paper, draw the outline of
the layout and apply the
colours to make a base
layer of red and blue.

Cover this whole area
with a thin layer of wet
paper pulp in a choice of
colours. Here pulp has
been used in its natural
beige colour and has also
been coloured red with
acrylic paint.

While the pulp is wet,
use the trowel's pointed
end to scratch away some
pulp to create a distressed
texture and reveal hints of
the base colours.

As a centrepiece for the
image, a paper stencil cut
in the shape of a star is
positioned on the layout.
Gold metallic powder is
applied to the stencil with
a brush, and red and
green metallic powders
are dusted around the
edges of the image. When
working with powders, tip
any excess onto a piece of
paper and pour it back
into the container.

Additional motifs are
pressed into the damp
pulp using stamps such as
screw heads or the
carved ends of sealing
wax sticks, creating
decorative borders. Dip
the chosen stamp in
metallic powder first - this
not only adds a metallic
finish but also stops the
stamp sticking to the pulp.

Finally, gently blow over
the finished piece to clean
away the fine residue of
powders.

4 USING SPRAY PAINT AND GLASS OUTLINER

EQUIPMENT

Sheet of tracing paper A3
   size (297 x 420 mm/
   11¾ x 16½ in)
Low-tack masking tape
Gold spray paint
Old newspapers, to
   protect worksurface
Gold tissue paper
Glue
Glass relief outliner

Working with the sheet of
tracing paper in a portrait
position, mask off three
evenly spaced, wide
horizontal bands using the
masking tape. Spray the
gold metallic colour onto
the exposed paper. When
using spray paint, work in
a well ventilated area and
protect your worksurface
with newspaper. Carefully
remove the masking tape.

Tear the gold tissue into
flower shapes and glue
them randomly onto the
stripes. To add dimension
and detail, paint an outline
over the tissue using silver
glass relief outliner,
applying it straight from
the tube.

METALLIC FINISHES

LEFT
This eye-catching, geometric piece, entitled *Gold Sun*, is by Danish artist Merete Zacho and made using lokta paper from Nepal. To achieve the striking finish, the paper has been painted with metallic paint and leaf. It measures 82 x 62 cm (32¼ x 24½ in).

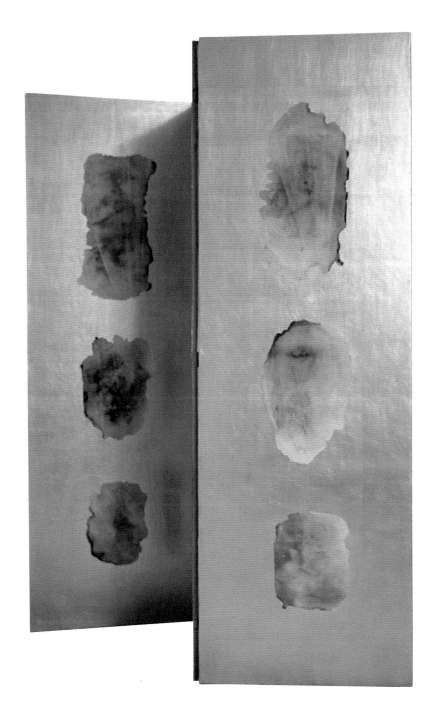

ABOVE

This exquisite dish by the British artist Hilary Bravo is made of plaster of Paris moulded on a metal plate, oiled and coated with pulp and then baked. The surfaces reflect the rough quality of the pulp which is coated with gesso and painted with acrylic inks.

BELOW

This piece by Katherine Virgils, entitled *Lapis Shrine*, was inspired by Mogul architecture and the colours of India. Papers were painted with bronze pigments and shellac, gold leaf and gesso and the layers combined as in a mosaic.

ABOVE

The Japanese designer Keiko Yamamoto has decorated this striking screen to achieve a vibrant metallic surface.

The surface is first coated with many layers of gesso. Once dry, it is smoothed with sandpaper and sealed with decol. The panel is gilded with aluminum leaf using gold size, then the image is applied. The three panels each measure 165 cm (65 in) in height and 55 cm (22 in) in width.

WORKING IN THREE DIMENSIONS

Paper, a two-dimensional material, can be transformed into three dimensions and converted into an infinite number of articles. For examples of this, we can look to the Japanese who still continue their long, inventive tradition of using paper to make a large range of household and recreational items, including lanterns, dolls, purses, kites and even kimonos.

Since its invention thousands of years ago, paper has been folded, trimmed and sewn together to make books. In this chapter we demonstrate an interesting form of Western-style bookbinding using some of the papers made, decorated and featured throughout this book.

Paper pulp can be sculpted, moulded and cast into low relief and made into, as well as applied onto, three-dimensional objects. When dry, the thick layer of fibres result in a form of three-dimensional paper with sculptural qualities. Pulp is used to dramatic effect in several of the techniques demonstrated here.

Right: This cabinet by Ann Frith has been magically transformed from a blank piece of furniture into a vibrant example of a functional sculpture with a distinct character and presence. The application of paint and varnish over a layer of paper pulp ensures a strong surface which will stand the test of time.

EQUIPMENT

Good quality waste paper

Scissors

PVA glue

Piece of untreated blank
  furniture

Offcuts of wood, to make
  the top platform

Wood or plaster filler

Parcel tape

Plywood

Hacksaw

Piece of dowel

Drill

Small wooden balls

Corro-flute or glue
  spreader

Paint brushes

Emulsion paint

Gold Schlag or Dutch Gold
  leaf

Wunda size or gold leaf
  size

Gloss and matt varnish

PAPIER MACHE

Papier mâché is a popular art practised by many craftspeople at different levels of expertise, from the school room all the way to the professional artist's studio.

There are two ways in which to produce this versatile material. Firstly, strips of paper soaked in a size solution can be applied to a mould to build up layers. The alternative method is moulding with paper pulp fibres. Readymade paper pulp can be purchased from good art and craft suppliers. A number of substances such as plaster and size can be added to the pulp to provide additional strength. The surface of the finished piece can then be polished or rubbed with sandpaper, painted and sealed with varnish.

When we think of papier mâché we nearly always picture a bowl. Although a popular choice of object, there are many other exciting ways that this raw material can be used. The demonstration featured here shows a simple piece of furniture transformed beyond recognition with the use of paper pulp, imagination and creative flair. The gallery on pages 132-133 also shows inventive uses of paper pulp.

2

3

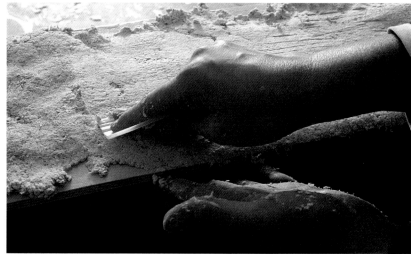

4

1 PREPARING THE PULP

Prepare the pulp using a good quality waste paper (shredded office paper is ideal). Full instructions on preparing pulp can be found on page 39.

To cover the cabinet shown in the photographs, you will need sufficient pulp to fill a standard sized washing-up bowl.

Once the paper has been blended into a fine pulp, mix with it with the PVA glue. Use about 2 cups of glue for a washing-up bowl of pulp.

Knead it into a clay-like paste, resembling dough, ensuring that the mixture does not become sticky.

2 CUSTOMISING THE CABINET

Simple untreated pieces of furniture known as 'blanks' can be transformed with the application of pulp.

Start by concealing unwanted features, such as the holes in the drawers as seen in the photograph. These have been backed with a short strip of parcel tape to provide a surface for the wood or plaster filler.

Begin to customise the piece by adding features such as the wooden platforms glued to the top of the cabinet.

3 APPLYING THE PULP

Working on one surface of the cabinet at a time, paint on a generous layer of PVA glue. While still wet, take a bundle of the pulp and press it firmly onto the prepared surface with the palms of your hands.

4 SMOOTHING THE PULP

Once the area has been covered with a thick layer of the pulp, scrape a flexible piece of card or corro-flute over the surface of the pulp, smoothing out the bumps and rounding off at the corners of the cabinet. The resulting layer should be no more than 5 mm (¼ in) thick.

For added interest, the pulp can be embossed with a decorative detail by pressing a piece of shaped card into the pulp while it is still damp.

Repeat the process until the whole cabinet has been covered and then leave it to dry thoroughly. Depending on the climate, this may take four to five days.

5

7

5 APPLYING DECORATIVE LEAF DETAILS

When the pulp has thoroughly dried, trace leaf patterns onto the surface of the cabinet with a pencil. Paint PVA glue on the marked areas. Taking a small handful of pulp, roll it between your hands into the shape of a sausage. Lay the pulp onto the glued area and pinch it into a ridged shape.

6

6 ADDING THE FLOWER

Cut out a plywood flower. Take a short piece of dowel and slice off half the thickness for a length of 2.5 cm (1 in) at one end. Lay this over the flower and glue together. Cover the flower's surface with pulp (as in step 2), then add a pulp pattern. When dry, decorate with gold leaf (as in step 7). Drill a hole in the top of the cabinet to hold the dowel and glue the flower in place. Glue the wooden balls onto the drawers.

7 APPLYING THE GOLD

When dry, paint the cabinet with emulsion. To mix your own colours, add coloured acrylic paint to white emulsion.

The schlag or Dutch Gold is supplied on a sheet in the same form as gold leaf. Paint the chosen areas with synthetic gold size, cut the leaf into strips and lay it on the glued areas. Rub gently to make the gold adhere to the surface. To prevent tarnishing, seal with gloss varnish. For contrast, the painted areas can be sealed with matt varnish.

PAPIER MACHE

ABOVE

Reliquary – The Branches of Life by British artist Deborah Schneebeli Morrell is constructed from laminated cardboard with relief work in papier mâché pulp, layered with paste-soaked sugarpaper. Five coats of gesso are applied, followed by several coats of acrylic paint and silver leaf. The figures inside the rooms are built up with pulp over a wire armature.

RIGHT

The designer Ann Frith uses papier mâché to make decorative objects such as boxes and mirrors. Her furniture pieces are constructed in medium density fibreboard onto which layers of pulp are applied, emphasising their organic shapes and sweeping curves. Ann decorates the surfaces with features sculpted in pulp and paints the pieces in rich jewel-like colours, embellishing the details with Dutch metal.

ABOVE

This lacquered set by British designerJessica Bourdon Smith is a very fine example of the application of papier mâché and gesso. The pots are finished with crackled lacquer and a final layer of polish.

RIGHT

This attractive gesso bowl is by British artist Kevin Ireland. The papier mâché is applied over a ceramic form, which is coated with gesso and copper inlay. It is finished with a final coat of gesso mixed with natural earth pigment. The piece is finished by sanding and sealing.

BOOKBINDING

The following technique of bookbinding is based on the Medieval practice of 'tacketing' where the cover was 'limp' or without boards and usually made from vellum. The sewing differs from the conventional hardback book where the 'sections' or folded pages are sewn together, often around a sewing support of cord or tape. The endpapers are sewn or tipped to either end of the book and are, in turn, stuck to the cover. The weakest point of this book is the joint of the cover and the endpapers. These often tear, causing the cover to part from the text pages. The tacketed construction shown here gives a book more strength and flexibility as the sections are individually sewn through the spine of the cover, eliminating the need for endpapers (though they can be used for decorative purposes).

An important factor is the 'grain' or direction of the fibres. This must run vertically on all paper and board used for covers and pages. If not, the paper will react to climatic changes. In time the text pages will ripple and the covers bow inwards or outwards, ruining the appearance of the book. Grain applies to mould-made and particularly machine-made papers where the majority of the fibres run along the length of the continual sheet. Due to trimming, it is not safe to assume the grain will automatically appear along the length of an individual sheet so the direction must be checked.

An experienced bookbinder is able to determine which way the fibres are lying simply by glancing over the surface of a sheet of paper. For the less experienced, gently bend the sheet without creasing it, first along the width and then along the length. In each case the top edge is bounced to test the resistance. As it will bend more easily along the grain, the direction is determined by which way the sheet is more flexible. The fibre direction of board can be checked in the same way.

EQUIPMENT

Paper for the sections
(here unprinted mould-
made Fabriano paper is
folded into six individual
eight-page sections -
see below)

Spine paper

Cover paper

Contrasting tissue paper

Sticky tape

Pencil and metal ruler

Scalpel and blade

Bone folder

Paper measuring strip

Compass

Set square

Fine bradawl or pin in
holder

Hammer

Copper wire

Thick linen or carpet
thread

Large needle

Thick card for back strip

Glue

Paper weight

1

A NOTE ON SECTIONS

The word section refers to
the pages of a book which
are folded at the spine.
These can appear in a
number of configurations,
for example a single
folded sheet is known as a
four-page section, if one
folded sheet is placed
inside another this
becomes an eight-page
section, and so on.

1 MAKING THE COVER AND SECTIONS

For the cover, select a
paper quite a bit larger
than the open page size.
Place the cover paper
face down and cut the
tissue paper for the lining.
This should run short by
about 1 cm (½ in) all round
so that when the cover is
folded over, the lining
does not sit proud. Attach

it to the corners with a
small strip of sticky tape.
The 'turn-ins', or parts of
the cover which are
folded over both top and
bottom and at the sides,
are first estimated by
laying down two sections
centred on the cover with
a space between them to
allow for the spine.

First, determine the
turn-in at the top of the

book (the 'head'). Mark a
pencil point on the cover
at the top right edge of the
section. Trace the
measurement from the top
edge of the cover on to a
paper measuring strip and
mark another point the
same distance down from
the top left of the cover.
Join the marks with a ruler
and using the sharp end of
a bone folder, crease a

line between the points.
Fold the cover and tissue
over by scoring a line
along the edge of the
ruler, bringing them up
against it. Then protect
the fold with some blotting
paper and burnish along it
using a bone folder to
avoid making the outer
surface of the paper shiny.

With the head folded
over, prepare to mark the
points for the bottom or
'tail' turn-in. From now on,
accuracy must be
maintained for a slick
result, and a paper
measuring strip and a
compass are used to
transfer precise
measurements.

Take all the sections
together (known as the
'block') and place on the
cover where the head is
folded over. Leave a small
space of no more than
2 mm (1/8 in) between the
top of the block and the
folded top edge of the
cover and mark a point
2 mm (1/8 in) below the
block. Remove the block
and fold the tail in the
same way.

2

3

4

2 MAKING SPINE FOLDS IN THE COVER

Estimate the final width of the spine by holding the block together loosely, making an allowance for the final sewing thread. Measure this area with a compass, transfer the measurement to the middle of the cover paper and make two marks across the head fold.

Use a set square to crease two vertical fold marks and fold the cover at these points. The turn-ins at each side of the cover are known as 'foredge turn-ins'.

Place the block against each spine fold and mark the points on the cover allowing a gap of approximately 2 mm (⅛ in). Crease and fold both foredge turn-ins.

3 MAKING THE COVER CORNER FOLDS

To make the corner folds, remove the text block and open out the turn-ins. Take one corner towards the centre of the book and fold it through the point where the head/tail and foredge turn-ins meet.

Complete all four corners in this way and then fold all the turn-ins back into place so that the diagonal edges of the folds meet. It is possible to reduce the bulk in the fold by slicing away a section of the corner within the head/tail and foredge folds and so conveniently remove the sticky tape.

4 SECURING THE COVER'S CORNERS

To secure the turn-ins, place a piece of thick, right-angled card inside one corner fold to protect the outer cover. Mark two points either side of the diagonal fold, measuring an equal distance with a compass. With a bradawl, make two holes and remove the card.

Cut a length of copper wire about 10 cm (4 in) long. Thread each end through the back of the holes and twist the wire into a coil. Flatten the coil with the flat edge of a bone folder and cut the loose ends. Repeat the process at each corner of the cover.

This copper wire has been tarnished for added visual effect by being heated to red hot over a flame and plunged into boiling water.

5 PREPARING THE COVER FOR SEWING

Mark the sewing points on the outer folds of the sections by placing the block flat with the spine facing outwards. Use a set square and pencil to draw four vertical lines with an equal distance of 1.5 cm (½ in) between the first and second lines and the third and fourth lines. The two bands should appear roughly equidistant, with the exception of the top band which should be nearer the top. It is common to set the bands on a spine closer to the top rather than centred as it is more visually correct.

Flatten out each section face down and pierce a small hole through the fold at the four points marked.

The outside spine of the cover features a backing strip with two decorative straps. To make the strip, cut a piece of thick card matching the length and width of the spine and cover it in a decorative paper. The cut edges may be painted in a contrasting colour for additional impact. Cut the straps from a thick decorative paper. These must be wider than the bands

5

6

drawn on the block in order to hide the sewing.

Lay the cover face up and place the block with the folded side close to the edge of the spine to determine the position of the straps. Glue the coverings face down across the spine so that they correspond with the bands drawn on the block. Glue the backing strip

onto the spine over the coverings and then place the cover under a heavy weight for five minutes.

To transfer the sewing points to the back strip, lay the cover face up with the block against the spine. With six sections, the backing would be weakened if six holes were punched across the width of the spine. The

solution is to make three and allocate two sections per hole. Mark the three points across the backing strip corresponding with each of the four bands on the block.

Place the cover face up on a piece of thick card and pierce through the backing strip, coverings and cover paper using a bradawl and hammer.

6 SEWING THE SECTIONS TO THE COVER

Cut twelve lengths of thread, each about 10 cm (4 in) long. Using the first length, begin to sew the sections onto the cover.

Thread the needle through the first hole in the backing strip, then through the top hole on the outside of the section, back out through the next hole down inside the section, and finally out through the corresponding hole in the cover. Pull the thread tightly so that the two ends emerging through the back strip are equal in length.

Secure the thread in place by tying two knots. With the first knot wrap the thread twice and pull it towards one of the holes locking it into place, then continue with the second knot. This ensures the first knot will not work loose.

Cut the excess threads and repeat this sequence with each section, sewing the top and bottom into place. Trim the coverings, wrap one side over the other and glue into place.

PAPER AS SCULPTURE

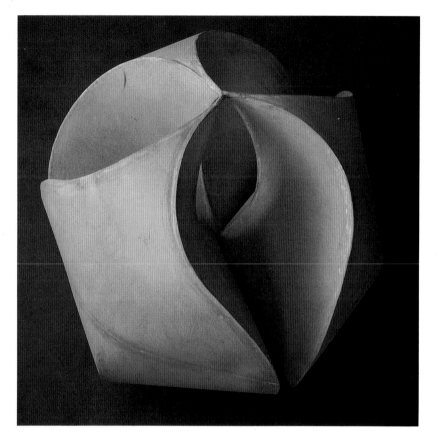

BELOW

The Inquisitive Pod, from a series of sculptures by the British artist Sarah Williams, is an exciting and striking piece based on the characteristics of exotic plant forms. A copper wire frame is constructed and covered with a layer of paper which is secured in place with PVA glue.

ABOVE

The Lotus Trinity by Kai Rentola, a Finnish artist, is made from three large, separate sheets of hand-made paper. This beautiful organic shape is completely hollow. The shapes are cut from the flat sheets of paper which are then carefully folded and glued together to create the unusual three-dimensional form. Tempera colour pigments are applied and the surfaces smoothed with sandpaper.

RIGHT

The Growing Growers, by the Swedish artist Margareta Mannervik, are constructed using sheets of paper hand-made with cotton rags, flax, reeds, hops, onions and banana skins. The shapes, arranged in an arresting composition, are mounted on lengths of iron tubing.

LEFT

This elegant sculpture, from a series by the artist and papermaker Mara Amats, is made using sheets of fine lokta tissue which have been laminated onto recycled soft drinks bottles. The material is cut, twisted and sculpted into a shape which evokes the natural forms of animal bones and skulls.

STENCILLING

The ever-popular technique of stencilling involves applying a motif to a given surface with the use of a mask which is usually made from paper or card, or sometimes a plastic sheet. An image is cut away from the stencil material, leaving spaces to be filled with pigment. This can be applied in a number of ways including the most common methods of spraying or dappling with a paint brush. The mask is then removed to reveal the image. In this way, the same motif can be repeated many times over a large surface area.

This is an ancient decorative technique, dating back to AD 650. In the monastic library found in the Tun-huang caves in northern China, the walls and ceilings had been stencilled with thousands of images of Buddha. The Chinese first used paper stencils carefully marked with tiny pin pricks to reproduce their simple designs.

In Japan this technique has been used since the eighth century in the dyeing of textiles. In Okinawa the method of stencilling paper known as *kata-zome* involving paste resist was developed. This was revived during the Second World War when cloth became a rare commodity.

Stencilling has been used widely throughout the history of interior design and decoration. In Britain, hand-made wallpapers which bore hand-stencilled patterns featuring heraldic shields and vases of flowers were in use by the end of the seventeenth century. In the middle of the nineteenth century, in Britain and America it was regarded as the height of fashion to stencil floors with geometric patterns resembling tiles.

Stencilling can be applied to a wide number of surfaces and can be used to decorate walls, doors, floors, picture frames and even fabrics. The following photographs show the technique being applied in a novel way as an image is built up with layers of coloured pulp spread onto card stencils,

creating a series of striking three-dimensional wall hangings. The pulp has been coloured ultramarine, red oxide and paynes grey by mixing it with paint and has been applied to pale grey paper.

Left: These fine pieces by Lynne Robinson and Richard Lowther are made by layering a choice of coloured pulp mixtures. The compositions are created by applying the pulp through card stencils.

EQUIPMENT

Reference book to show
    letter forms/leaves
Photocopies of
    letters/motifs to size
Stencil card
Low tack repositonal glue
Cutting mat and scalpel
Foamboard
280 ml (10 fl oz)
    readymade pulp
Artists' acrylic paint or
    artists' powder pigment
in three colours
Sheet of hand-made paper
    approximately 300 x
    560 mm (18½ x 35 in)
Pencil
Ruler
Bowls or tiles for mixing
    pulp
Spoons
Palette knife or spatula
Plastic film
Lino roller or wooden
    rolling pin

1 PREPARING THE STENCILS AND PULP

Photocopy the chosen images and motifs to the required size. Stick all the copies except the larger letter to stencil card with the glue. Cut out the stencils with a scalpel.

Stick the larger letter lightly to a sheet of foamboard with the glue and cut out the stencil with a scalpel, angling the blade down into the areas to be cut away (the stencil hole should be slightly wider at the bottom than the top to making lifting it off the pulp easier).

To make pulp from recycled paper, follow the guide to preparing pulp for simple papermaking on pages 38-39. Alternatively, buy readymade pulp to which water is then added (available from specialist papermaking and craft suppliers).

Make up three lots of pulp, each mixed with a different colour. To colour the pulp, add either artists' acrylic paint or artists' powder pigment.

1

2

2 CREATING THE STRIPES

Place the sheet of plain paper in a portrait position. Draw in two pencil rules to mark out a wide stripe about one-third of the way down the sheet. In the photograph here, a brick red pulp is used and spread between the lines using a trowel. The pulp should be applied to make a layer 2-3 mm (⅛ in) thick.

3 SMOOTHING THE PULP

Apply plastic film over the wet area and with a rolling pin, roll out the pulp to smooth over any lumps. It is important to press lightly so that the pulp does not stick to the plastic film. Use a lino roller or a wooden rolling pin (a marble one will be too heavy).

4 APPLYING THE LEAVES

Before the first layer of pulp dries, lay the leaf stencil onto the stripe and apply another coloured pulp (blue is used here).

Using a palette knife or spatula, fill the cut away areas with pulp and roll it out gently, just to press into into the coloured stripe. If you are too heavy-handed, the colours will bleed into each other.

Leave the pulp to dry thoroughly. This can take a day or two, but to speed up the process, leave in a warm place, such as an airing cupboard.

3

4

5

5 APPLYING THE FINAL MOTIF

Taking the foamboard stencil, lay it over the whole area and tape down the corners. The board can be further secured by weights or simply held in place by pressing down with one hand. Using the palette knife or spatula, apply the third layer of grey pulp, filling the cutaway section of the stencil. Roll out the pulp very gently, as in step 4.

CREATIVE CORRUGATE

BELOW

The body of this free-standing Mantle Clock by Nigel Cripps of ID8 Design is made entirely of corrugated card and comes in a flat pack form ready to be assembled using tabs and slots. The piece is made from two types of corrugated card. The main body and face are made of double faced 'E' flute and the pillars from single faced 'E' flute. The term 'flute' refers to the width of the ribs while 'face' refers to the amount of layers which make up the card.

RIGHT

The American designer Roland Simmons uses corrugated card to create sculptural shapes of unique beauty. These elegant Lumalights, from the Babylon Design collection, are excellent examples of his work. The fine white corrugated paper is scored with geometrically calculated lines, creating bold structures beautiful in their simplicity. The lights range in size from 1 m (3 ft) to over 2 m (7 ft).

ABOVE

The French artist Amélie Dillemann of Carton Massif stretches the use of cardboard to its limits, recreating familiar objects in this versatile material. This handbag and door are made from cardboard using glue and scissors. The handbag is an original design in natural coloured card, while the double door is in an eighteenth-century style.

ABOVE RIGHT

This piece, entitled *Little Beaver*, designed by the architect Frank O. Gehry, is part of a limited series known as *Experimental Edges*. It forms part of the Vitra Edition, an armchair with an ottoman made of cardboard with a specific wave and thickness. Templates are made and different layers of cardboard are then cut and glued together to form the final structure.

BELOW

This set of miniature cardboard furniture entitled *Famille Carton* was designed by the French architect Olivier Leblois, whose life-size furniture has sparked wide interest in London, France and New York. Leblois believes that cardboard furniture contributes to the conservation of the ecological balance of the planet. The hollow and isothermal nature of the corrugated cardboard reproduces the heat of the environment, making its surface warm and pleasant to the touch. The pieces shown here are scaled to ⅛ life size.

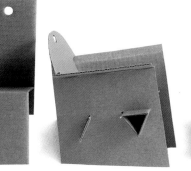

MOULDING

Pulp is a versatile substance which can be sculpted over an infinite number of objects and textures, slavishly taking on the shape of the original as it shrinks and dries. In this way, paper can reveal the exquisite beauty of simple everyday surfaces which are often overlooked.

Experiment with different objects and surfaces - anything from a basket weave to a stone carving or even a common rubber car mat. As seen in the photographs here, these can create the most intriguing textures when impressions of pulp are taken from them. In the demonstration shown on page 148, a fish fossil is moulded to create a negative paper copy, retaining all the fine detail with remarkable accuracy.

Paper mouldings can be objects of great beauty in their own right. Many accomplished artists produce paper-moulded pieces on both large and small scales and exhibit them widely to great acclaim. Moulded paper can also have a practical application, such as being used for the cover of a notebook or photo album, as well as providing decorative elements, such as on a gift card.

A choice of two techniques is presented here, one involving the use of a mould and the other using a sieve. Before you begin, choose a waterproof worksurface. As liberal amounts of clean water are required when following these techniques, ensure that you have plenty of absorbent cloths and sponges at hand to mop up overflowing water.

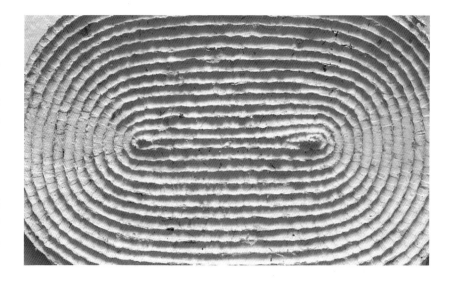

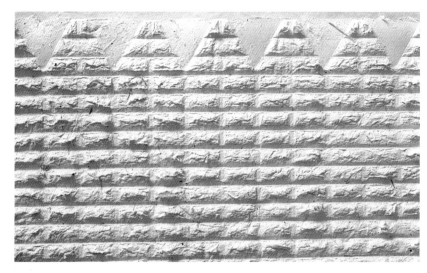

Top: When applied to a chosen surface and allowed to dry, wet paper pulp will take on the shape of a given surface. The paper shown here is the dried result of the pulp moulded in step 1. The texture of the basket weave with all its intricate detail is slavishly recreated in the pulp.

Above: The paper featured here is an example of how interesting surfaces can be created using the most unlikely objects, such as a rubber car mat. This is the paper made in step 2.

1 MOULDING USING A SIEVE

Place the object on which you intend to mould next to the paper and water-filled vat. In this demonstration a wicker tray is used. With a flat sieve, scoop up a generous amount of pulp from the vat and slap it onto the chosen surface.

Gradually build up the layers until the whole object is covered in a blanket of pulp no less than 2 cm (¾ in) thick.

Place a cloth over the surface of the pulp and press down to squeeze out as much excess water as possible, ringing out the cloth as you repeat the process. This action also compresses the fibres, resulting in a stronger structure.

1

2

EQUIPMENT

Vat of pulp and water mixture

Flat sieve

Cloths and sponges

Choice of objects on which to mould

2 MOULDING USING A PAPERMAKING MOULD

The pulp fibres may also be applied with the use of a papermaking mould.

Make a sheet of paper by gathering the pulp on the mould face in the usual way (see pages 45-47) and couch the layer of fibres straight onto the chosen surface.

3 PEELING OFF THE MOULD

The layer of pulp may take a few days to dry completely, depending on the temperature and humidity. It is best to dry it naturally to prevent the pulp from shrinking too much. If you require fast results, a microwave oven can be used. However, avoid using any metal utensils and never leave it 'cooking' unattended.

Once completely dry, carefully peel the mould away by first picking away at the edges, gently freeing it from the surface, to reveal an exact negative of the original.

3

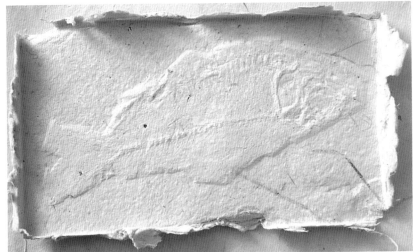

Left: The surface details of three-dimensional objects can be successfully recreated in gentle relief using pulp. This paper mould, taken from the stone carving shown above, demonstrates the surprising effectiveness and versatility of paper pulp.

Above: Wet pulp is applied to this fish fossil to demonstrate how the finest detail can be translated into a layer of paper pulp.

EQUIPMENT

Vat of pulp and water
    mixture
Plaster in powder form
Bone carving or chosen
    relief object
PVA medium
Fine sheet of tissue paper
Clear varnish or non-
    water-based paint
    (optional)

CASTING

Casting is the name given to the method of pouring molten metal into a negative mould in order to reproduce a relief or three-dimensional object, a technique traditionally employed by sculptors and model makers. The common choice of material used to make negative moulds (plaster, rubber or various metals) depends on the media from which the final object is to be cast. Although paper pulp is not often thought of in the serious sculptural tradition, it can be successfully cast in a flexible negative mould such as one made of rubber and cloth.

In this sequence a mould is made using paper pulp, creating a paper replica of a Tibetan carving. This piece is made from bone, originally from a Shaman's apron.

1 MAKING THE MOULD

To prepare the material for making a negative mould, mix a quantity of pulp, depending on the size of the intended mould, with the same quantity of plaster powder added to it. The plaster acts as a setting agent.

Choose an object which is in relief and apply the thick pulp mixture around it, gradually building up the layers. When it is about 1 cm (½ in) thick, leave it to dry (this can take several days, depending on the thickness of the layers).

When thoroughly dry, carefully separate the mould from the original piece, making sure that it does not tear. Coat the inside of the mould with a waterproofing substance such as a PVA medium. This ensures the cast piece does not adhere to the mould. Leave to dry.

2 CASTING FROM THE MOULD

Line the inside of the mould with a fine sheet of wet tissue and fill the cavity with a thick pulp mixture, compacting it into all the spaces.

It may take a few days for the pulp to dry depending on the temperature and humidity. It is better to leave the mould to dry naturally, rather than speeding up the process by placing the mould on a radiator or in an airing cupboard, as this would encourage the pulp mixture to shrink.

Carefully remove the cast paper piece from the paper mould, revealing a direct replica of the original. If you wish, seal the cast with either clear varnish or a non-water-based paint.

CAST AND MOULDED PAPERS

LEFT

This beautiful composition is made up of a number of mouldings reproduced in paper pulp, from maize and recycled paper, by the artist and papermaker Mara Amats. The top section has been moulded onto a woven Gambian fan while the paper below shows the impression of a Tibetan monk's writing table. The pulp is dyed using indigo to achieve the subtle muted tones. The mouldings are presented on a sheet of hand-made lokta paper.

ABOVE

This fine piece entitled *Cloct Barn*, by the British artist Carol Farrow, is made from paper cast on wood. The fibres making up the sheet are derived from cotton linters. The casting is then painted with acrylic and finally waxed, to evoke the characteristcs of the original surface.

BELOW

The British artist Lesley Davy utilises natural elements to create her paper castings. This piece, named *Sea Level* and made with hand-made paper from cotton linters, was cast on a beach. The texture and surface of the sand are faithfully recreated with an added detail of rust.

RIGHT

This fine piece by American artist Kay Stowel is from a collection of paper mouldings taken from the Roman city of Pompeii where on 24th August AD79 everything was frozen in time. Seeing the rich colours and crumbling walls inspired her to create her Pompeii series. She processed pulp from a variety of plant materials, dyeing and moulding it onto the columns and sections of walls of the city.

RIGHT

These reliefs by the American artist Seena Donneson are unique works of hand-made paper. The pulp is saturated with colour, embossed and textured, then moulded and assembled or collaged against a canvas or museum board. The materials used are linen pulp, gelatin, and ascorbic acid. Plaster of paris is used as a size and the colour is water-based and ground from powdered pigment.

CONTRIBUTORS' BIOGRAPHIES

Mara Amats

Demonstrated the papermaking techniques and variations, sizing, embedding, moulding, casting, embedding with pulp and embossing on pages *38-55, 86-87, 90-93,* and *146-149.*

Mara Amats was born in Latvia and educated in France and Canada. In 1959 she came to England to study art under Sir Lawrence Gowring. In the early 1960s she returned to France and apprenticed herself to iconographer Gregory King at the monastery where she had grown up. Her work there gave rise to an invitation to restore icons and frescoes in the Coptic churches of Ethiopia. This led to the first of many years of travelling and working among the poorest craftspeople, initiating income generation schemes. She has installed paper projects in the Caribbean, India, Nepal and South Africa, using plants indigenous to each area.

Andrew Bennett

Demonstrated the technique of folding and pleating on pages *70-73.*

Andrew Bennett studied Graphic Design at The Royal College of Art. While pursuing a career in design, he quickly turned his attention to his main fascination, paper engineering. He has spent many years experimenting with paper and perfecting his technique. Andrew is able to achieve a high level of accuracy in his work with the use of 2D and 3D computer graphics programs which he has customised to meet his specific needs. He has designed many elaborate paper sculptures and written several cut-out books, among them *The Paper Hat Book* and *Animal Masks.*

Ann Frith

Demonstrated the technique of papier mâché on pages *128-131.*

Ann Frith studied Sculpture at Brighton College of Art. She went on to a post graduate teaching course and became Head of Art at a school in Shropshire, England. Four years ago, Ann embarked on a worldwide trip across Asia and the Far East. It was in India that she was inspired by papier mâché and on her return to England began to experiment. She has taken the medium to a new level of sophistication, with her range of ornamental boxes, frames and furniture. Ann has completed various commissions including designs for a restaurant and garden and, most recently, a grand chaise longue and matching cabinet for a client in Vienna. Colour plays a vital role in her work, and the jewel-like blues, pinks and turquoises of her pieces are reflected in her working environment.

Sandra Grantham

Demonstrated the technique of Japanese wood block printing on pages *110-113.*

Sandra Grantham studied Paper Conservation at Camberwell College of Art before going on to complete a PhD on a Royal College of Art/Victoria & Albert Museum Joint Conservation Course. Her research is being carried out at the Victoria & Albert Paper Conservation Department. Her particular interest is Japanese pigments and all forms of Japanese art. Sandra recently won The Royal College of Art Award for student exchange with Kyoto City University of Arts, Japan, where she conducted three months of study and research into Nihonga, a form of classical Japanese painting. During this time she visited three papermaking villages where she formed sheets in the traditional manner. She met the last remaining Karakami printer in Kyoto, Senda-san, who is the eleventh generation of a family of Karakami printers and produced prints using blocks from his precious collection.

Richard Lowther and Lynne Robinson

Demonstrated the techniques of stencilling and applying metallic finishes on pages *122-125* and *140-143.*

Lynne Robinson and Richard Lowther have worked together since moving to France in 1989. Lynne originally studied fashion design and fashion illustration. Established as a freelance illustrator in 1976, her drawings have been commissioned by magazines, publishers, advertising agencies and design groups. She has also been a tutor at Epsom College of Art and a visiting lecturer at a number of other art schools. Richard studied fine art. Although specialising in sculpture, his work encompasses painting, drawing and print-making and he has exhibited his work widely. Whilst living in London, he taught at West Surrey College of Art, Epsom School of Art and the London Institute, Chelsea College. On his move to France, he taught at Parsons School of Design in Paris for two years. Today, their partnership produces paintings, design work, decoration, painted furniture and illustration for clients in both England and France.

Ron Macdonald

Demonstrated the technique of making and sewing a watermark on pages *56-59.*

Ron Macdonald has been making watermarks, dandy rolls, moulds and deckles since 1948. He began his five-year apprenticeship at the time when his father, Mr H.C. Macdonald, and two colleagues took over the business originally set up by Edwin Amies in 1793. The company, based in Maidstone, Kent, has a portfolio of prestigious work including watermarks for many international banks and special commissions for the monarchy. Under the name of Edwin Amies and Son, Ron Macdonald produces handcrafted bespoke moulds, deckles and watermarks in the traditional manner. He has inherited an impressive collection of historical wax carvings, casts, masterplates and watermarked papers. Papermakers from as far away as the Far East, Africa, Australia, New

Zealand, North and South America as well as Europe continue to employ his talent and rare expertise.

Jane Millar

Demonstrated the technique of collage on pages *94-97*.

Jane Millar is a graduate of The Royal College of Art where she studied painting (tapestry) and incorporates textile techniques in her paintings and paperwork. She now teaches textile art and painting at Winchester School of Art and at the University of West England, Bristol. As an additional activity, she has begun to produce exquisite one-off collage pieces with much commercial success. Her clients include the Conran Shop and a selling exhibition at Sotherby's, plus private commissions.

Romilly Saumarez Smith

Demonstrated the technique of tacketed bookbinding on pages *134-137*.

Romilly Saumerez Smith originally studied paper conservation and went on to specialise in book-binding at Camberwell School of Arts and Crafts. In 1978 she became the first woman employed to bind books at the Zaehnsdorf Bindery in London. Romilly has taught the subject at a number of institutions,

including Guildford College of Technology, London College of Printing and Camberwell School of Arts and Crafts. She balances her time between private tuition and prestigious commissions for collectors, artists, private presses and many distinguished authors, among them Michele Roberts, Salman Rushdie and George Mackay Brown. She has work displayed in many public collections, including the V&A, The British Library, The Crafts Council, The New York Public Library and the Humanities Research Center in Texas. Romilly is on the Crafts Council Index and is a Fellow of Designer Bookbinders, and has exhibited her work widely over the years.

Deborah Schneebeli Morrell

Demonstrated the techniques of decorative markings and paste painting on pages *64-67* and *106-109*.

Deborah Schneebeli Morrell studied Fine Art at Bath Academy of Art at Corsham. She uses mixed media to make her sculptural pieces, often drawing her influence from the folk art traditions of European and Central American cultures where the art is deeply rooted in everyday life. Deborah has

taught widely in many colleges and schools and, more recently, has contributed to over twenty books, acting as sole author on a further ten, writing and devising projects covering a wide range of crafts. When asked to describe her work, she says that she likes to make it look as if it has always existed.

Solveig Stone

Demonstrated the technique of marbling on pages *114-119*.

Solveig Stone worked in advertising for Young and Rubicam as an Assistant Television Producer before travelling to America in 1969. Here she saw an exhibition of Cobden Sanderson hand-marbled papers and was captivated by the technique. On her return to England in 1972, she sought the advice and expertise of the late Sandy Cockerel, who encouraged her and showed her the rudiments of the craft. Largely self-taught, she later became the marbler at Compton Press in Wiltshire. Solveig registered her own company, Compton Marbling, in 1979 and won a Design Council Award for her work. Over the years she has continued to perfect her skill and refine the process, stating that 'nothing in marbling is random'.

Beata Thackeray

Demonstrated the techniques of fold and dye, tie-dye and crumpling on pages *80-83* and *100-105*.

Beata Thackeray graduated from The Royal College of Art in 1988. She has since worked at The Body Shop International as senior accessories designer. Beata has travelled to Asia and Eastern Europe, working with producers of paper, wood and textile products. Driven by her belief in the principles of ethical trading, she has worked with fair trade producers in Nepal and India and, most recently, with a papermaking group in Bangladesh, where she has trained women in the skills of product development. Beata has long been involved with hand-made paper, assisting in the creation of unique papers using plants indigenous to developing economies. Using these papers, she has designed numerous products for sale in Western markets. This is her first book.

Michelle Wild

Demonstrated the technique of weaving with paper yarn on pages *76-79*.

Michelle Wild completed an MA in Woven Textiles at The Royal College of Art. In 1991 she travelled

to Taiwan where she taught woven textile design at The Fu Jen University in Taipei. She now lectures at a number of colleges including the Nottingham and Trent University and Central St Martin's. Michelle acts as a creative consultant for commercial weaving manufacturers and also takes on prestigious site specific commissions for clients such as Belsay Hall in Northumberland. Since 1993 she has worked as a self-employed designer/maker selling work internationally to numerous clients, including Ulf Moritz of Sacho Hesslein, The Conran Shop, David Champion Int and Jack Larsen.

Terry Perkins

Kindly demonstrated making the simple mould and deckle on page *37*.

SOURCES AND SUPPLIERS

Suppliers of Papermaking Equipment and Materials

Edwin Amies and Son Ltd
33 Amsbury Road,
Coxheath, Maidstone
Kent ME17 4DP
Telephone: 01622 745758
Makers of moulds and
deckles, dandy rolls and
watermarks. Contact: Ron
Macdonald

Ellison Universal Press
Fords Farm, Winston near
Stowmarket, Suffolk
IP14 6BD
Telephone: 01728 861018
Manufacturer of bench-
top presses. Contact:
Philippa Ellison

Kilkie Paper Mill Services
Melville Square, Comrie,
Perthshire PH6 2DL
Telephone: 01764 670141
Suppliers of second-hand
papermaking equipment.

Suppliers of Hand-made Papers and Artists' Materials

Fred Aldous Ltd
P O Box 135, 37 Lever
Street, Manchester 1,
M60 1UX
Telephone: 0161 236 2477
Fax: 0161 236 6075
Mail order craft materials.

L Cornelissen & Sons Ltd
105 Great Russell Street,
London WC1B 3RY
Telephone: 0171 636 1045
Artists' supplies.

Falkiners Fine Papers
76 Southampton Row,
London WC1B 4AR
Telephone: 0171 831 1151
Stocks a variety of hand-
made papers.

General Paper Industries
Manufacturers of hand-
made paper and products
in Nepal. For information
call their London contact:
0181 886 6164 or e-mail:
kbr86@dial.pipex.com

JvO Papers
15 Newell Street, London
E14 7HP
Telephone: 0171 987 7464
Maker and supplier of
conservation papers.
Contact: John van
Oosterom

Paperchase
213 Tottenham Court Road,
London W1P 9AF
Telephone: 0171 580 8496
Stocks a variety of hand-
made papers.

Papeterie
35 Market Place, Kingston
upon Thames, Surrey
KT1 1JQ
Telephone: 0181 546 0313
Supplier of hand-made
papers. Contact: Jo
Bessey

Specialist Crafts Ltd
P O Box 247, Leicester
LE1 9QS
Telephone: 0116 251 0405
Fax: 0116 251 5015
Mail order craft materials.

The Two Rivers Paper
Company, Pitt Mill,
Roadwater, Watchet,
Somerset TA23 0QS
Telephone: 01984 641028
Quality watercolour paper.
Contact: Jim Patterson

Twinrocker Hand-made
Paper Mill
P O Box 413, Brookston,
Indiana IN 47923, USA
Telephone: (317) 563 3119

Udyog Hand-made Paper
Project
Manufacturers of hand-
made paper and products
in Bangladesh. For details
call their London contact:
0181 886 6164 or e-mail:
kbr86@dial.pipex.com

Wookey Hole Mill
Wookey Hole, Wells,
Somerset BA5 1BB
Telephone: 01749 672243
Suppliers of hand-made
paper; working museum.

Suppliers of Machine-made Papers

Arjo Wiggins Fine Papers
Turpin Lane, off Manor
Road, Erith, Kent DA8 2AT
Telephone: 0800 993300

British Paper Company
Frogmore Mill, Mill Street,
Apsley, Hemel
Hempstead, Hertfordshire
HP3 9RY
Telephone: 01442 231234
Manufacturers of 100 per
cent recycled papers.

Curtis Fine Papers Ltd
Guardbridge Mill, St
Andrews, Fife KY16 0UU
Telephone: 01334 839 551

Spicers Ltd
Sawston, Cambridge
CB2 4JG
Telephone: 01223 834555

Associations and Sources of Information

Barcham Green & Co Ltd
Hayle Mill, Maidstone,
Kent ME15 6XQ
Telephone: 01622 692266
Historical and
contemporary paper
consultants. Contact:
Maureen Green

British Association of
Paper Historians
64 Nutbrook Street,
London SE15 4LE
Contact: Peter Bower
Quarterly journal and
other reference books.

Estamp
204 St Albans Avenue,
London W4 5JU
Telephone: 0181 994 2379
Publisher of books on
papermaking and
printmaking. Contact:
Silvie Turner

Paper and Pulp
Information Centre (PPIC)
Papermaker's House,
Rivenhall Road, Westlea,
Swindon SN5 7BD
Telephone: 01793 886086

Victoria & Albert Museum
London SW7 2RL
Telephone: 0171 938 8500

Environmental Groups

Greenpeace International
Stichting Greenpeace
Council, Keizersgracht 176
1016 DW Amsterdam,
Netherlands
Telephone: 31 20 523 6200

Women's Environmental
Network
87 Worship Street, London
EC2A 4BE
Telephone: 0171 247 3327

Artists and Designers working with Paper

Crafts Council of Great
Britain
44A Pentonville Road,
London N1 9BY
Telephone: 0171 278 7700
For details of artists
working with paper.

Andrew Bennett
c/o David Higham
Associates Ltd, 5-8 Lower
John Street, London
W1R 4HA
Telephone: 0171 437 7888
Design and paper
engineering.

Compton Marbling
Lower Lawn Barns,
Tisbury, Salisbury,
Wiltshire SP3 6SG
Telephone: 01747 871147
Maker and supplier of
hand-marbled papers.
Contact: Solveig Stone

Ann Frith
5 Chesham Street,
Brighton BN2 1NA
Telephone: 01273 625365
Papier mâché artist.

BIBLIOGRAPHY

Richard Lowther and Lynne Robinson
29 rue de l'Homme de Bois, 14600 Honfleur, France
Telephone: 02 31 89 44 41
Artists and designers.

Papel sin Fronteras
Knudrisgade 29 1, DK-8000 Arhus C, Denmark
Telephone: 45 86 12 99 38
A group of European artists working with paper.

Romilly Saumarez Smith
13 Newell Street, London E14 7HP
Telephone: 0171 987 4943
Bookbinder.

Deborah Schneebeli Morrell
10 York Rise, London NW5 1SS
Telephone: 0171 485 4261
Artist.

Something Strange
71 Venn Street, London SW4 0BD
Telephone: 0171 498 9295
Painter and collage artist.
Contact: Jane Millar

Thackeray Design
13 Selborne Road, London N14 7DD
Telephone: 0181 886 6164
or e-mail:
thackeray@dial.pipex.com
Graphics and product design.

Michelle Wild
76 Kew Road, Richmond, Surrey TW9 2PQ
Telephone: 0181 332 2993
Weaver and textile design.

Books

Timothy Barrett : *Japanese Papermaking - Traditions Tools and Techniques*, Weatherhill, 1992

Sophie Dawson and Silvie Turner: *A Hand Papermaker's Source Book,* Estamp, 1995

Jules Heller: *Papermaking*, Watson-Guptill Publications, 1978

Sukey Hughes: *Washi*, Kodansha Int Ltd, 1982

Dard Hunter: *Papermaking - The History and Technique of an Ancient Craft*, Dover, 1978

Jacqui Hurst and Martina Margetts: *Classic Crafts*, Conran Octopus, 1989

Eric Kenneway: *Complete Origami*, Ebury Press, 1987

Rosamond B Loring: *Decorated Book Papers*, The Harvard College Library, 1973

Austin Pilkington: *Frogmore and the First Fourdrinier - A History of the British Paper Company,* Laurence Viney Ltd, 1990

Neeta Prenchand: *Off the Deckle Edge*, The Ankur Project, 1995

Maureen Richardson: *Plant Papers*, 1987

Lynne Robinson and Richard Lowther: *Stencilling*, Conran Octopus, 1995

Bo Rudin: *Making Paper - A Look into the History of an Ancient Craft*, Rudins, 1990

John Sweetman: *Making Paper by Hand*, an extract from *Appropriate Technology* reprinted by Wookey Hole Mill, 1982

Paper as Image, The Arts Council of Great Britain, 1983

Reports and Briefings

Renate Kroesa: *The Greenpeace Guide to Paper*, Greenpeace International, 1990

Pauline Webber: *The Parkes' Collection*, The Paper Conservator, Volume 15, 1991

Paper - How It's Made and What It's Used For, A Spicers Ltd Self Instruction Booklet

Recycling: The Greenpeace View, Conservation Papers Ltd Newsletter, Issue 2, 1990

Talking Conservation, Issues 9, 10, 11 and 16, Conservation Papers Ltd

Pulp Fiction; The Truth about Paper and the Environment., Raw Material - the Publication for Print, Design, and Production, Arjo Wiggins, 1996

Green Technology and the Computer User, conference organised by Conservation Papers Ltd, 1993

Green Paper 92 - A Review of the UK Market for Recycled Printings and Writings, sponsored by Conservation Papers Ltd, 1992

Paper Round - A Report on the Trend Towards Recycled Paper in British Business, sponsored by Wm Sommerville and Sons, 1991

Packaging and The Environment, Women's Environmental Network Briefing, 1991

Forests, Paper and the Environment, WEN Briefing, 1992

Alternative Fibres, Paper and the Environment, WEN Briefing, 1995

The WEN Guide to Waste and How to Prevent It, WEN Briefing, 1996

Recycling Paper, Paper Factfile no 1, Pulp and Paper Information Centre, 1993

Environmental Labelling, Paper Factfile no 2, PPIC

Packaging, Paper Factfile no 3, PPIC

News Paper, Issues 5, 6 and 7, PPIC

Paper and the Environment - A Summary, Paper Naturally, PPIC, 1990

Arjo Wiggins Environmental Report, 1996

Curtis Fine Papers Environmental Report,1995

GLOSSARY

Agitating The action of stirring the slurry in the vat to keep the fibres suspended before making a sheet.

Beating The action of breaking down plant matter into fibres by extracting the non-cellulose matter.

Block printing Applying ink to a design carved in a block of wood and transferring it onto paper.

Bookbinding Folding sheets of paper and sewing them into sections which are then bound inside an outer cover.

Cartridge paper A heavyweight uncoated paper for watercolour artists and painters.

Casting Pouring a wet paper pulp into a casting mould to make a relief or three-dimensional paper replica of a chosen object.

Coated paper A paper with a coating applied, giving it a smooth surface, making it less absorbent and more suited for fine quality print.

Cotton linters A papermaking ingredient made up of the short fibres which cover the seeds of the cotton plant.

Couching The process by which a wet layer of fibres is transferred from the mould face to the felt.

Creasing Running an implement over a surface of paper to compress the fibres, making the sheet easier to fold.

Crumpling Treatment applied to a paper to give the surface added texture.

Dandy roll A large cylinder used to create watermarks in machine-made papers.

Deckle The wooden frame held against the mould during the making of a sheet containing the fibres on the face of the mould.

Deckle edge The rough outer edges of a sheet of hand-made paper, created by the deckle.

Embedding Inserting a decorative element into fibres of a sheet during the papermaking process.

Embedding with pulp Combining various pulp mixes to create one layer of fibres which bond to form single sheet.

Embossing Impressing an image or texture into the fibres of sheet of paper so that they appear in relief.

Face The wire mesh covering the mould.

Felt A woven or felted blanket of wool or natural fibre onto which the wet layer of fibres is couched.

Fibres The substance resulting from the process of beating and pulping a papermaking ingredient. The matter from which a sheet of paper is formed.

Fold and dye Folding a piece of paper into a concertina and dipping the corners into a dye to create decorative patterns

Folding Turning a sheet of paper over and smoothing it to leave a flexible bend in the fibres.

GSM Weight measure of paper, ie grams per square metre.

Hollander beater A pulping machine invented in Holland to break down fibrous matter into a pulp.

Itajime-zome Japanese art of fold and dye.

Laid A wire face of a mould woven in a pattern giving the paper texture.

Marbling Floating patterns of paint onto a surface of size and transferring them onto paper.

Masterplate A mould cast from a wire frame motif used to duplicate a watermark design.

Mould The wooden frame stretched with a wire mesh on which a sheet of paper is formed.

Moulding Applying a layer of wet pulp onto a surface to gain an impression.

Papier mâché Using paper strips soaked in size or a pulp mixture to coat a surface resulting in a hard layer of sculpted paper.

Paste painting Applying paint onto the surface of a paper and working patterns into it when wet.

Post A mound of couched sheets ready for pressing.

Press A device used to extract water from layers of couched fibres. Also used to flatten dry sheets.

Pulp A collection of macerated fibres derived from a number of sources including recycled paper, wood or plant matter.

Scoring Marking a paper by making a slight incision across the fibres, making paper easier to fold.

Shibori-zome The Japanese art of tie-dye.

Shifu The Japanese art of weaving with paper.

Size A starch or gelatin solution added to the papermaking process, making the sheet less absorbent.

Slurry The mixture of pulp diluted with water from which a sheet is formed.

Suminagashi The Japanese art of marbling.

Tie-dye Tying a material and winding thread around to create a circular pattern when it is dipped into dye.

Tissue paper A soft crepe paper used for decorative and domestic purposes.

Vat The container in which the pulp mixture or slurry is kept.

Washi Hand-made Japanese paper usually made from one or more plant fibres (kozo, gampi and mitzumata).

Waterleaf Paper which is not treated with size.

Watermark An image seen in paper when held to the light, created by a feature on the mould face.

Weaving Passing yarns through each other to create a piece of cloth.

Wove A wire face of a mould which gives the resulting paper a smooth texture.

INDEX

PICTURE CREDITS

The publishers wish to thank the following photographers, agencies and craftspeople for permission to reproduce their work:

6 -7 Thomas Kelly; 8 Paul Thackeray; 10 The British Paper Company; 11 Jacqui Hurst/Conran Octopus; 12 top, middle & below Courtesy of the Board of Trustees of The Victoria & Albert Museum; 13 Courtesy of the Board of Trustees of The Victoria & Albert Museum; 14 Beata Thackeray; 15 Thomas Kelly; 16 Barcham Green & Co Ltd, Hayle Mill; 17 Paul Thackeray; 18 Beata Thackeray; 23 The Image Bank/Gabriel Covian; 24 - 25 The Paper Federation of Great Britain; 27 Vibeke Bak Hansen; 68 left Joanne McCrum/Off The

Wall Lighting; 68 right Georgia Scott; 69 above Mette Grue-Sorensen; 69 below Ann Vilsboll; 74 left Nel Linssen (Photograph: Peter Bliek); 74 above right Reiko Wanibuchi; 74 below right Nel Linssen (Photograph: Peter Bliek); 75 left Mary Butcher (Photograph: Jacqui Hurst); 75 right Mary Ann Lomonaco (Courtesy of the American Crafts Council); 86 above Lois Walpole (Photograph: Jacqui Hurst/Conran Octopus); 86 below Clare Goddard (Photograph: Andra Nelki, courtesy of Cratfspace Touring); 87 above Annette Meyer; 87 below left Heidrun Guest (Photograph: George Carter/Conran Octopus); 87 below right Marian Smit; 92 above Mildred Fischer (courtesy of the American Crafts Council); 92 below Lin Fife (courtesy of the American Crafts Council); 93 above left Val Fox; 93 above right Val Fox; 93 below John Babcock; 98 above Mark Hill (Photograph: Jacqui Hurst/Conran Octopus); 98 below Caroline Burzynski-Delloye (Photograph: Jacqui Hurst/Conran Octopus); 99 left Sarah Hamilton (Photograph: Jacqui Hurst/Conran Octopus); 99 right Beata Thackeray (Photograph: Jacqui Hurst/Conran Octopus); 117 below Compton Paper Marbling (Photograph: Jacqui

Hurst); 120 below Compton Paper Marbling (Photograph: Jacqui Hurst); 120 above Colleen Gryspeerdt (Photograph: Jacqui Hurst); 120 below Compton Paper Marbling (Photograph: Jacqui Hurst); 121 Victoria Hall (Photograph: Jacqui Hurst/Conran Octopus); 126 Merete Zacho; 127 left Keiko Yamamoto; 127 above right Hilary Bravo (Photograph George Carter/Conran Octopus); 127 below right Katherine Virgils; 132 left Deborah Schneebeli-Morrell (Photograph: Heini Schneebeli); 132 right Ann Frith; 133 above Jessica Bourdon-Smith; 133 below Kevin Ireland (Photograph:George Carter/Conran Octopus); 138 above left Kai Rentola; 138 below right Sarah Williams; 139 above Margareta Mannervik; 139 below Mara Amats; 144 left Nigel Cripps; 144 right Roland Simmons; 145 above left Amelie Dillemann (Photograph: Rene Stoeltie); 145 above right Vitra Design Museum (Designer: Frank.O. Gehry); 145 below Quart De Poil (Photograph: Jacqui Hurst/Conran Octopus); 150 left Mara Amats (Photograph: Jacqui Hurst/Conran Octopus); 150 right Carol Farrow; 151 above Kay Stowell; 151 below left Lesley Davy; 151 below right Seena Donneson.

AUTHOR'S ACKNOWLEDGEMENTS

Thank you to the contributors for allowing me into their studios, sharing their knowledge and expertise and for their help with the text: Andrew Bennett, Ann Frith, Sandra Grantham, Richard Lowther, Ron Macdonald, Jane Millar, Lynne Robinson, Romilly Saumarez Smith, Deborah Schneebeli Morrell, Solveig Stone, and Michelle Wild. A special thank you to Mara Amats.

I would like to thank the following specialists and experts in the field of papermaking who generously assisted me with my enquiries and requests: Maureen Barcham Green, Terry Gurden, Jim Patterson, Robert Waller and Pauline Webber. Also my gratitude to Milan Dev Bhattarai, Intermediate Technology (ITDG) Bangladesh, Socio Economic Development Society (SEDS) Bangladesh and British Executive Service Overseas (BESO) UK.

A big thank you to the team: Denny Hemming, Gillian Haslam, Jacqui Hurst, Alison Fenton, Jess Walton and Jo Alexander. I enjoyed every minute.

Finally I wish to thank my husband Paul for his endless support, advice and encouragement throughout.